THE
DECISION
MAKER

Also by Dennis Bakke

Joy at Work

Unlock the Potential
of Everyone in
Your Organization,
One Decision at a Time

THE
DECISIN
MAKER

DENNIS BAKKE

BESTSELLING AUTHOR OF *JOY AT WORK*

Pear
Press

Pear Press
P.O. Box 70525
Seattle, WA 98127-0525
U.S.A.

This book may be purchased for educational, business,
or sales promotional use. For information, please visit
www.pearpress.com.

FIRST EDITION

Library of Congress Cataloging-In-Publication has been applied for.

ISBN-10: 0-9832633-2-9

ISBN-13: 978-0-9832633-2-6

To Eileen Harvey Bakke,
the love and joy of my life,
and the best friend
anyone could ever have

Contents

Introduction

Nothing tells you more about an organization than the way it makes decisions.

Do leaders trust team members? Do the people closest to the action get to make the call? Do team members have real responsibility and real control? All of these questions can be answered by one other one: who gets to make the decisions?

And nothing affects an organization more than the decisions the people in it make.

Great business minds know this. In fact, decision-making is at the heart of all business education. Nearly a hundred years after the case-study method was invented at Harvard, it's still the foundation of the world's best business programs. Why? Because the case-study method puts top business students in the role of decision-maker. Over the course of a Harvard MBA, students will make decisions on more than 500 cases. Decision-making is simply the best way in the world to develop people. And real-life decisions are more important—and more fun—than any case study.

But outside of business school, few business leaders tap into the value created by putting important decisions in the hands of their people. Instead, "team players" are taught to do what they're told. This takes the fun out of work, and it robs people of the chance to contribute in a meaningful way. Or, organizations will use a participatory style of decision-making in which recommendations are given to the boss, who then makes the final decision. This approach also fails to fully realize the value of the people in the organization. What I am talking about is quite different. In a decision-maker company:

• the leader chooses someone to make a key decision

• the decision-maker seeks advice (including from the leader) to gather information

• the final decision is made not by the leader, but by the chosen decision-maker.

At AES, an energy company with 27,000 people in 27 countries, and at Imagine Schools, one of the country's largest non-profit charter school networks, I have had the good fortune to give thousands of people the freedom and responsibility to make decisions that matter. The idea is simple: treat people like people, not machines. When leaders put control into the hands of their people, at all levels, they unlock incalculable potential.

The Decision Maker is a fable, loosely based on my own story, that shows how the ideas that transformed AES and Imagine Schools can transform any organization. The events are fiction, but the passion, purpose, moral questions, and common sense are rooted in decades of my own experience. These ideas can affect the bottom line: cutting-edge research indicates that a decision-maker culture improves financial performance. But it's not just about the numbers. It's about people: what makes them tick, and what they can achieve when they're given real responsibility and real freedom.

One other thing: *The Decision Maker* is founded on the idea that all of us can make good decisions. So this story is not just for people who currently lead organizations. It's for managers at any level who want to unlock the full potential of the people around them.

No matter where you stand in your organization, change can start with you.

1.

How Bad Is It?

Tom Anderson could see the smoke rising from the manufacturing floor long before he reached the site of the explosion. But even the clouds of steam that belched from the broken machine couldn't prepare him for what he saw when he got there.

The machine wasn't just broken. It seemed to have been obliterated. Through the rolling mist, he could make out a gigantic hole flanked by twisted metal. Shards of glass crunched under his feet.

His partner, Jim Travers, was there already. He looked up as Tom approached.

"How bad is it?" Tom asked.

Jim shook his head. "This one's a total loss," he said. "We're insured against that. But we're not insured against this."

Tom followed his gaze. Almost miraculously, none of the equipment nearby had been damaged in the explosion.

But none of it was working. And neither were their people, who stood in clusters in the aisles, talking amongst themselves.

Columns of numbers began to run through Tom's mind. He and Jim had taken over the medical device company only two weeks ago. They'd sunk everything they had into it. Helen Harris, one of the savviest private-equity investors in their field, had financed the rest, based on Tom and Jim's successful track record as managers at a similar operation—one where they'd had no ownership at all. Their business plan was aggressive but lean. Tom knew it couldn't withstand a shutdown for long.

Jim sighed. "Well, at least no one got hurt."

A shock went through Tom. He'd been so worried about the broken machinery that their people's safety hadn't even crossed his mind. But despite his relief, he had trouble believing no one had been injured.

"Are you kidding?" he said, gesturing at the hunks of machinery beyond the steam. If metal couldn't withstand the blast, what chance would a person have had? "What was he wearing, body armor?"

Jim shook his head. "He wasn't here."

Tom's heart sank. He and Jim had known MedTec had some problems with morale when they took it over. In fact, they'd seen those problems as an opportunity. The staff and product were both strong; they just weren't being used to their fullest potential. Once Tom and Jim came in with their superior management techniques, they'd see higher productivity from the same people. At least that's how the theory went. Their business plan involved changes they hoped would put them in the running for some regional "best employer" awards. They'd already put a pair of vintage pinball machines in the employee lounge, installed a micro kitchen, and started providing healthy snack foods free of charge. But it looked like they had a problem here that went deeper than games and snacks could solve.

"Why not?" Tom asked. "Where was he?"

"Doing what he was told," Jim said. "He caught the indicators right away. He knew something was wrong. So he went to get his shift supervisor."

"Thank God he wasn't there," Tom said.

"Yep," Jim said.

"He didn't know how to shut it down on his own?" Tom asked.

"Oh, no," Jim said. "He probably knew better than anyone in the plant. He does it at the end of every shift. But he wasn't authorized. Only the manager could shut it down mid-shift."

"And in the meantime, the machine blew."

Jim nodded.

Tom let out a long breath. "That's crazy," he said.

"You're telling me," Jim said.

Tom glanced around at the clusters of workers in the aisles. One man glanced back at him and then quickly averted his eyes, as if he was worried any contact with the boss might lead to trouble. Tom recognized the look. He'd given it to countless bosses himself.

"Look at them," Tom said.

"I've been trying not to," Jim said. "Every hour they're idle costs us thousands of bucks."

"That's not what I'm talking about," Tom said. "I mean, look at them."

Jim looked around. "What?" he asked after a minute.

"They look like us," Tom said. "Before we bought this business. They're just trying to keep their heads down and get through the day without the boss interfering too much. They've even got that look we were starting to get."

"What look?"

"The glazed one," Tom said. "The one you get from checking your mind at the door when you come to work."

Jim crossed his arms and shook his head. "Maybe you're right," he said. "But I've got to get a technician in here to fix this thing. Or find us a new machine, preferably for free. I don't think the mood of our employees is our biggest worry at this point."

"Maybe not," Tom said, as Jim headed down the aisle back to the main office.

But as Tom followed Jim, it wasn't the broken machine that stayed stuck in his mind. It was the faces of their people. They knew how to get a machine into good working order, even if it was an expensive hassle. But people weren't machines. They were a lot more complicated, and they didn't come with a simple handbook.

What about them? he wondered.

2.

Lipstick on A Pig

As soon as Tom stepped onto the manufacturing floor the next morning, a stocky, silver-haired man in a blue work shirt strode down the main aisle toward him. Tom recognized Ben Malkmus, the area manager, and lifted his hand in greeting.

Ben gave a tight smile as Tom walked up. "Tom," he said. "What can I do for you?"

Tom gave him a hearty handshake. "How are you doing?"

"We're doing," Ben said. "We've got everything running we can. But the machine that went down is pretty crucial to our operation."

"I understand that," Tom said. "And I understand the tech running it identified a problem before it blew."

Ben's expression turned guarded. "None of this was his fault," he said. "Anton's a good tech. He was following protocol."

Tom nodded. "I'm not worried about Anton," he said. "I'm worried about the protocol. He knew how to turn the machine off, but he didn't."

"I didn't make the protocol," Ben said. "That all came down from HR."

Ed Harkness, the previous owner, must have been one of those bosses who always wanted to know whose fault it was, Tom thought. Ben could barely talk about fixing the problem. He was too busy defending himself and his people from blame.

"Well, I'd like to talk with you about how it's been working," Tom said. "Because it didn't seem to work very well for us yesterday."

"What do you suggest?" Ben asked, crossing his arms.

"I want our people to have the power to make decisions that are good for the business. Like turning off a machine when they can see it's in trouble."

"You're talking about giving them the power to shut down the whole line," Ben objected. "Workers can't always see the big picture like the manager can."

Tom nodded. "Sure," he said. "But if Anton had had that power yesterday, the line would be up and running this morning."

Ben couldn't argue with that, but he didn't seem to like it. "I'm just not sure what the point of having a manager is," he said, "if the manager doesn't make decisions."

"We are making a decision," Tom said. "We're deciding that we might not be the best one to make every decision."

"You're the boss," Ben said.

That wasn't the point Tom was trying to make, but he let it pass for now. "Is Anton around?" he asked.

"This way," Ben said. He led Tom through the maze of machinery to a station where a tall black man was inspecting a batch of metal parts. He looked up when he saw Ben. "I think we can use most of these," he said. "I've been checking the specs, and it looks like the parts were good right up till it blew."

"Anton," Ben said. "This is Tom Anderson. The new owner," he added.

The same wariness Tom had seen in Ben's eyes now appeared in Anton's. Anton laid down the part he'd been measuring and faced Tom, his shoulders squared.

"I want to thank you," Tom said.

Startled, Anton glanced at Ben. Ben shrugged.

"We know it's not your fault the machine blew," Tom continued. "It's ours. You did the right thing by trying to save the machine. If we'd given you the power, you could have. The next time you see something like this coming, I want you to go ahead and shut it down."

Anton's expression turned a shade cynical. "That's easy to say now," he said. "But what if I'd shut down the machine and it didn't blow? Then you'd be down here asking me how come I'm holding up the whole line."

"That's when you'd tell us you held up the line to save the machine," Tom told him.

Anton raised his eyebrows, unconvinced.

"Is there anything else?" Ben broke in. "We've got a lot going on today."

"That's it," Tom told him. "For today."

Tom headed back to his office, unsettled. The culture of control and blame at MedTec seemed to run deeper than they'd thought. And neither Ben nor Anton seemed thrilled about his attempt to address the problems.

On the way back, he stopped off in the employee lounge. This, he thought, he could be proud of. Just as he'd hoped, a trio of people was gathered around one of the handsome vintage pinball machines. When Tom joined the group, the woman across the machine greeted him with a friendly smile, and the man beside him gave a half nod.

They didn't recognize him, Tom realized. It was a small company, but big enough that not everyone knew each other. He'd been there for only a couple of weeks. And they probably didn't expect to see the company owner in the employee lounge.

When the game finished, he couldn't resist.

"Pretty nice, isn't it?" he said. "Harkness never gave us a lounge like this."

The guy who'd just finished playing was thirtyish, with sandy blond hair that fell just below his chin—probably one of the researchers, from the looks of him. The look he gave Tom was half amusement, half disbelief.

"Lipstick on a pig," he said.

Tom's eyebrows shot up. "What do you mean?"

"Oh, come on," the guy said. "The pinball machines. And did you see the announcement they've got up now? The Friday night parties they want to start?"

Tom nodded. The Friday night parties had been his idea.

Sure, pinball machines were nice, but he wanted to build real camaraderie within the company and show his people how much he valued them. Regular parties, he figured, would do both. And put all the improvements in the lounge to good use.

"Smoke and mirrors," the guy said. "They wouldn't have to give us all this stuff if it wasn't such a terrible place to work."

Tom glanced at the pinball machine, stung.

The woman checked her watch. "We're gonna be late," she said.

The guy stepped back from the pinball machine and spread his hands toward it. "It's all yours," he said as the group filed out.

Back in his office, Tom's administrative assistant, Vanessa Dominguez, greeted him with a big smile. "Good morning," she said.

Tom started to pass her, preoccupied. Then he circled back. "Vanessa," he said. "You seem happy."

Vanessa's pretty, middle-aged face turned puzzled. She'd been prompt and accurate with answers to his other questions about the business, but she didn't seem sure about the right answer for this. "I'm happy," she said, her voice tentative.

"You're happy to be here?" Tom said. "Happy at work?"

The puzzled look vanished from Vanessa's face. Her smile widened.

Tom felt some of the stress slide from his own shoulders. At least one person at MedTec seemed to like her job.

"Oh, Mr. Anderson," she said, beaming. "You don't have to worry about that."

Tom smiled back.

"I never expected to be happy at work," Vanessa added.

"Wait," Tom said. "So you're not happy *here*?"

"I'm happy when I'm at home," Vanessa said. "With my family. This job lets me take care of them."

"But you're not happy here," Tom insisted.

Vanessa laughed and handed him a pink sheaf of phone messages.

"Work's not supposed to be fun," she told him. "That's why they call it work."

Instead of going straight to his own office, Tom took a detour to Jim's. Jim was seated behind the giant mahogany desk they'd inherited from Harkness when he left. He leaned back when Tom came in.

"I just came from the floor," Tom said.

Jim grinned. "I just ran the numbers," he said. "If they can get the machine back up in the time they promised, we'll still hit our projections for the month. Just." He let out a sigh of relief. "I wasn't looking forward to telling Helen we'd missed our goals the first month out."

"I think we've got a problem here," Tom said.

The grin vanished from Jim's face. "Not another equipment malfunction," he said. "I can't believe it. All this stuff was just inspected as part of the sale."

"It's not the machines," Tom said. "It might be worse."

In tough times, Jim was always able to buckle down, take the truth, and move on. It was one of the things Tom liked best about him—and one of the reasons he trusted him. Now he could see Jim compose himself, his eyes alert, waiting for the worst. "What?" he asked evenly.

"The people here," Tom said. "They're not happy."

Tom could see Jim's eyes flicker. He was trying to take Tom seriously, but Tom could see Jim didn't rate this as a problem on the level of a major equipment malfunction.

"Well," Jim began. "We knew we had some problems with morale coming in. But we're not going to manage the same way Harkness did. And once they find the new lounge, and start coming to your parties—"

"I think the lounge is actually part of the problem," Tom said. "They think it's smoke and mirrors, to hide the fact the jobs are rotten."

"Who's 'they'?" Jim asked.

Now that Tom tried to put his concerns into words, they seemed thin, even to him. But the fact that he couldn't put the feeling into words didn't make it go away. If anything, his unease grew as he struggled to express it. "Everyone I talked to," he said. "None of them seem happy. It's not what we wanted when we decided to go into this. We wanted our own business, something we could run our way. And we wanted our people to be happy, too. We didn't want to be the only ones in the building who got to do what we liked to do."

"You can't make everyone happy all the time," Jim reminded him.

"But *nobody* here seems happy now," Tom said.

"Listen," Jim said. "I'd like to have a satisfied workforce as much as the next guy. For one thing, there are a lot of economic incentives to pay attention to employee satisfaction. People like a place, they work harder, waste less. I'm not going to argue with any of that. I just don't think it's our central concern. Not at this stage in the game."

"It's a central concern to me," Tom said. "Harkness has been treating these people like machines. They're not machines, so they're not happy. But it's not just about their happiness. When they can't turn off distressed equipment, the whole line goes down for days. That's a genuine business outcome for us."

Jim raised his eyebrows.

Tom recognized the look. They'd worked side by side for years. They had a healthy respect based on that. But they didn't always see eye to eye. And sometimes, they'd realized, one of them just needed some time to work a problem out on their own.

"Well," Jim said. "What would you like to do about it?"

Tom wished he had an answer. Right now, all he had were questions.

"I'll get back to you on that," he said.

3.

The Big Game

"Paid breaks," Tom said, listing the advantages of life at MedTec to his wife over the squeak of sneakers and slap of the basketball on the court where his son Jason played below. "A fantastic lounge. We actually pay them to play pinball. I'm not sure what more someone could ask. I would have thought I'd died and gone to heaven if someone had given me a job with a pinball machine in the employee lounge."

Sophia, his wife, gave him one of her sidelong glances. The wry twist of her lip made him remember why he'd first fallen for her. It also let him know a zinger of some sort was coming. "Are you kidding?" she asked. "How much time have you spent down in that lounge since you took over MedTec?"

As the boys on the court barreled from one hoop back to the next, Tom's eyebrows drew together. "I haven't had time," he said. "We've had all kinds of things to do. You wouldn't believe the number of decisions we've had to make. There's a lot of pressure."

Sophia nodded. He could tell she'd just swapped caps—from basketball mom to consultant. Tom had first met her when she led a team that helped reorganize his department years ago. Her keen business mind was still in demand, and she still took on projects that interested her, even though she'd scaled back her professional responsibilities in the intervening years. "Would you rather have been playing pinball?" she asked.

Tom thought for a moment. "No," he admitted. "But—"

Sophia's gaze shifted to the court. "Shh," she said. "Watch."

Out on the court, the game had been hard fought. The teams were well matched, and they'd traded the lead all night long. Now the score was tied. In the last scramble for a shot, one of the players on the opposing team fouled as the clock ran out. Tom's son, Jason, was handed the ball, and he stepped to the free-throw line.

Tom felt a knot of fear in his gut. He'd been complaining about pressure, but he wasn't a high school kid about to try for the game-winning point in front of everyone in his school. Jason was a good player, but he was new on the varsity team this year. How would he hold up?

Everyone watched Jason anxiously—the coaches, the refs, his team members. When Tom looked at Jason's face, though, it was concentrated and confident. Jason was totally focused, in a world of his own. He looked, Tom realized, like the happiest guy in the place.

Around them, the crowd fell silent. For a moment, nobody

seemed to move. Jason planted his feet firmly at the free-throw line, then took his shot. The ball arced through the air and dropped through the net with a barely audible swish.

Tom and Sophia leapt to their feet along with the rest of the crowd. A roar of victory thundered through the court. Tom caught a glimpse of Jason, grinning in triumph, as the jubilant crowd streamed down from the stands.

Tom and Sophia congratulated Jason and followed the flow of the crowd out to the parking lot. Tom still couldn't get the look he'd seen on Jason's face, the moment before he took the shot, out of his head. It should have been a hard spot to be in: serious pressure, with serious consequences. So why had Jason looked so happy?

The answer struck him as he was opening the car door for Sophia. Jason had been happy because he had the ball. For that one moment, he was the only person in the gymnasium who had control over what was about to happen.

And Sophia was right. That was a whole lot more fun than playing pinball in the employee lounge.

"You're right," he said after he circled back and took the driver's seat.

"About what?" Sophia asked, in a tone of voice that suggested she was right about so many things it was hard for her to guess what he might be referring to.

"It's fun to have the ball at the crucial moment," Tom said. "And that doesn't happen for our people at MedTec. That's why Anton couldn't shut off the machine before it blew. Because we didn't let him have the ball."

He pulled out of the parking lot. "We need to let our

people make decisions about the things that really affect them. They're the ones on the line. They're the ones who understand the research and the manufacturing. They know best, not us. We need to free their hands so they're able to make the shots that count, when they matter the most."

"That sounds great," Sophia said, and reached for his hand.

Tom closed it in his own with a strong sense of relief. The problem his mind had been grinding through all weekend had finally unwound.

"It's amazing," he said, warming to his topic. "People think work is hard and sports are fun. But I bet nobody at MedTec this week got to do anything as challenging as what Jason just did. And Jason was having a blast. He loved being the guy with the ball when it really mattered."

"That's the problem," Tom continued. "We're the coaches, but we've been trying to play the game, too. You don't see the coaches dribbling up and down the basketball court. That's not what they're supposed to do. They choose the players to send in. And then they stand back and let the players play the game. You can't tell a player what to do every single play. It'd ruin the game."

The more he thought, the more positive outcomes he saw. "Giving decisions to our people will make us more efficient, too," he said. "I bet waste will go down if we give them responsibility for materials in their own areas. It'll improve morale. It'll—"

"What do you think it'll be like for you?" Sophia said.

"For me?" Tom glanced at her face as the headlights of a

passing car slid over it. "It'll be great. Why wouldn't it? Wait. What do you mean?"

"You love to make decisions," Sophia told him.

"I—" Tom started. "I do?"

Sophia nodded. "You love to come home and tell me you decided on this, so now there's a whole new product line coming out, or you decided on that, so now everyone gets an extra day of vacation. You even like to decide things at home. When we order pizza, it's an exercise in strategic planning."

"Not all pizzas are the same," Tom protested.

"All I'm saying," Sophia said, "is that if you let your people make more decisions, there won't be as many left for you."

"Hm." Tom stared out the window as he piloted the car between the high school and home, turning this over. He was willing to give Sophia her point. Maybe he did like to make decisions. But that only proved his bigger point: people were happiest when they had the ball, when they were in a position to make the decisions that affected their world.

By the time he pulled into the driveway, a full-fledged plan was blossoming in his mind—one that he was pretty sure would solve the problems he'd been wrestling with at MedTec, and perhaps even more.

Sophia shrugged out of her wool sweater and hung it up in the hall. "I'm going to read for a while," she said. "You coming up?"

He kissed her and shook his head. "I'll be along in a minute," he said. "I've just got a few things I want to jot down."

As she disappeared through the kitchen, he headed down the basement stairs to his home office. He sat down at his desk, pulled out a clean sheet of paper, and began to write.

4.

That's Your Decision

"This isn't exactly just a new pinball machine for the employee lounge," Jim said, looking up at Tom from behind his desk. His expression clearly was skeptical.

"Exactly," Tom said. "It's a whole new way of doing things. That's what you and I wanted to do when we bought this place. And that's what this place needs."

Jim shook his head. "I'm not sure I agree," he said. "The growth here has slowed, but the numbers are still strong. In this economy, that means something. And much as I like your basketball metaphor—"

"It's not just in basketball," Tom said. "The game is like life. Life is like the game."

"Right," Jim said, with the tone of forbearance he used when he was waiting for Tom to come back to earth again from one of his visionary flights. "But Tom, there's a reason not everyone in a company makes the big decisions. Not everyone has been trained in this stuff. And not everyone has the experience."

"They don't have it because we never give it to them," Tom countered.

"Look," Jim said. "Say this was the best idea in the world. We're still easing into our leadership roles here. We've got a fiduciary responsibility to our investors, and they signed on for MedTec as it stands, not for some grand experiment in changing the face of the way we do business. I don't think this is the time for a big change. Especially not one that could have a negative effect on profit."

"But these problems are costing us *now*," Tom insisted. "We're not going to hit the first-quarter numbers we could have because Anton wasn't allowed to make the decision to turn off his machine."

Jim tilted his head, giving him the point, so Tom pressed on.

"And profits aren't the point of doing business," he said. "They're like breathing. You have to have them to stay alive, but they're not your reason for living. Not for us, anyway. We never just wanted to make a quick buck. We wanted to do something that mattered. Make something the world needs. We wanted to run a place where people like to come to work. If it was just about the money, we could still be clawing our way up the corporate ladder, pulling down fat paychecks and taking a whole lot less risk to get them."

"Sure," Jim agreed. "But there are nice ideas, and then there's good business sense."

"This is good business sense," Tom said. "A lot has

changed since we went to business school. People used to love to focus on the bottom line because you could count and measure it. But money isn't the best motivator. For anybody. People want all kinds of things money can't buy. They want time with their family. They want to enjoy what they do. They want to feel like they're part of something meaningful. They want to make something that matters, too. They don't just want to get paid. They want to live a good life. And when we tap into that, we release all kinds of productivity and efficiency—because our people care about what they're doing, and they're working for something they really want."

"It doesn't sound that efficient to me," Jim said. "We've got the expertise to make the decisions. The efficient thing is for us to make them, not to give them to someone else."

"We didn't have the expertise to shut down Anton's machine," Tom said. "And we didn't have the information to know we should have, even if we'd had the expertise. Anton's manager didn't even have that expertise and information in the moment that it mattered. Anton did. And if he'd had the ability to make that decision, we'd still be up and running.

"It's just like a basketball game. A coach can't play all the positions at one time. He can't even tell each player how to play the game. He coaches the players and chooses who to send in. But he can't play the game for them."

"You've reminded me of that a couple of times now," Jim said.

"Come on, Jim," Tom said. "We've got a chance to make MedTec anything we want. You know what it's like to work in a place where no one but the boss ever makes a decision. Do you really want MedTec to be one of those places?"

Jim gazed across the desk. Tom could tell he'd struck a chord. The two of them had forged their friendship at a big national corporation with a classic top-down model. It wasn't just that a few top people made all of the decisions there. Sometimes it seemed virtually impossible to tell who had made a decision at all. The experience was numbing, and stifling. Both Tom and Jim had watched deals fizzle and business relationships wither when they couldn't get answers in time from higher-ups. And when higher-ups could be bothered to hand down answers, they often didn't understand the situation well enough to make a good call.

Even worse, it was next to impossible to run a good idea up the chain. Sure, there was a process in place for "innovation"—just like there was a process for everything else, from filing expenses on up. But the fact of the matter was that it required months of wrangling and multiple permissions from company leaders who might or might not know how a given area truly worked before anything could move— which meant many things never did.

So most people in the organization treated the idea of innovation as a joke. Everyone knew you didn't move ahead by trying something new. The cost of failure was just too high. Instead, you kept your head down and put in your time, and eventually someone gave you a raise and a promotion.

Tom and Jim had met because they'd both been crazy enough to try to push forward new ideas they'd come up with. Tom's idea had been visionary: he'd seen an opportunity for a new product that he believed could be rolled out with existing staff and current capacity. Jim's idea had been, like Jim, relentlessly practical. In his spare time, he'd developed a system to eliminate inefficiencies in materials flow on the manufacturing side that he estimated could save the company millions.

While they waited to meet with the same executive, they'd gotten to talking in the reception area. Both of them had immediately seen the potential in the other's idea. And both of them had been glad to meet someone else who still had the fire to innovate.

The executive hadn't been quite as enthusiastic. He listened politely to Tom's idea for the new product, then told him he was skeptical: would it be feasible without interrupting the current workflow? Tom showed him graphs he'd created on logistics and said his manager was willing to do a test run. But when Tom asked for the chance to produce a sample, the executive balked, saying the company wasn't in a financial position to gamble on unproven product.

Jim's idea, because it was pitched as a money-saver, got more traction. But when the executive agreed to a test run, he insisted Jim run everything by him. Then he was chronically unavailable to hear Jim's progress reports or make the decisions Jim needed in order to move forward. For the next six months, Jim and Tom kept in touch as Jim's project limped along.

Then a competitor came out with a product almost identical to the one Tom had unsuccessfully pitched. The company lurched into a competitive frenzy that killed Jim's project, too. The executive's excuse was that the company couldn't afford to focus on anything that wasn't a core competency as it scrambled to meet this new threat in the market.

Tom's and Jim's ideas had been good ones. Maybe even great ones. But Tom and Jim hadn't been in a position to make the decisions.

It was when his project was killed that Jim finally started to seriously consider Tom's dream of leaving the company to run another business together. And it took two more years for them to find the right one: MedTec. But it was the desire to make important decisions, to have some control, that had brought them here. And Jim knew it.

He sighed and lifted his hands from the desk in a "you got me" gesture. "You're right," he said. "I don't want MedTec to be one of those places. But I don't want to take it under with some crazy scheme, either.

"I'll tell you what. You go ahead and try this new idea. That's your job. I'll watch the bottom line. That's mine. And if what you do in your job starts to affect mine, we'll need to have another conversation."

Tom grinned. "How will that conversation go if the numbers start going up?"

Jim suppressed a smile. "Make them go up, and we'll talk.

"And I won't be the only one who's watching," he added. "Helen Harris is going to have her eye on our books as well. And she's about as sharp as they come."

"This is about a whole lot more than profits," Tom said.

"Maybe," Jim agreed. "But we don't have a company without them."

"But you're willing to try," Tom prompted. "That's your decision."

"That's my decision," Jim said.

5.

Basic Assumptions

Tom surveyed the crowd gathered in the MedTec lounge. When he'd asked Vanessa to plan the all-company meeting, they'd discovered it was the only place in the business big enough to hold everyone. Now almost two hundred people were seated at the dozen or so tables, standing in the rows between them, or clustered in the back, around Tom's prized pinball machines. A handful of managers and team leaders sat in the front seats, watching warily. Tom and Jim had met with them to discuss Tom's ideas before rolling them out to the company. Tom had done his best to respond to their concerns and questions over the past few weeks, but his management team still didn't exactly look enthusiastic.

"What do you think?" Tom said to Jim, his voice low.

"I think it's eleven o'clock," Jim told him. "And this is an eleven o'clock meeting."

"Okay," Tom said. "Wish me luck."

"It's gonna take a lot more than luck," Jim said, as Tom stepped to the podium.

"Good morning," Tom said. He scanned the faces that turned to him as the microphone squealed with feedback. Some were curious. Some seemed annoyed their conversations had been interrupted.

"I'm here this morning to talk with you about some changes we'll be making in the coming days at MedTec."

At this, the traces of curiosity in the crowd began to vanish. About half the people glanced at the ceiling, out the window, at each other. Even the expressions of the ones who still looked at him closed up. He knew the signs. They were settling in, getting lost in their own thoughts, preparing to wait him out.

He looked down at the notes he'd scrawled the night of Jason's basketball game, and pressed on.

"Most companies," he said, "treat their workers like children."

Around the room, a few heads swiveled back to look at him.

"What are the basic assumptions of the modern workplace?" he asked. "We've got a lot of rules, because we assume people can't think on their own. We've got managers and consequences to keep us in line, because we assume people are going to break the rules we give them. We aren't supposed to color outside the lines. We're always supposed to ask for permission. We take grown people, and we treat them like kids. Not even like good kids. Like kids we're pretty sure can't be trusted."

All eyes were on Tom now. He even saw a few nods in the back of the room.

"What that means," he went on, "is that the bosses end up with all the decisions. We talk a lot about teamwork. But in most of the business world, the people who should be coaching are actually trying to play all of the positions. People think that sports are fun and work isn't. But that's not because sports are easy. Players make a lot more decisions in a single basketball game than a lot of people get to make at work during a whole day. That's what makes sports fun. The coach puts you in the game. And then they actually let you play."

He hadn't lost anyone's attention. But out in the crowd, he could see people beginning to think: come up with objections, decide whether they agreed.

"It can be a lot of fun," Tom said, "to be the guy who's got the ball on the line for a game-winning free throw. Not because there's no pressure. Not because there are no consequences. But because the decision is yours. And even if you're not the type to want the ball in the last second of the game, there's still a lot of fun in being on the team, setting a screen to set up the shot, or dishing the ball to another player for the winning shot.

"Here at MedTec, we want to put our players in the game. We're still going to coach. But we're going to do what coaches are supposed to do. Prepare our team to play the best games of their lives. And have a great time while they're playing.

"So we're not going to operate on those old assumptions here at MedTec," Tom said, gathering steam. "Here's what we believe about our people. What we believe about you."

He moved from the podium to the whiteboard behind him and began to scrawl out the notes he'd first taken in his basement office.

"We believe you're unique," he said, writing the word out as he spoke. "With different strengths and different needs. We believe you're creative, thinking individuals. We believe you're capable of learning. We believe you're capable of making decisions."

He looked up from the list. "We believe you like a challenge." A few people exchanged glances at this one, as if he might be trying to pull a fast one on them. "We believe you're capable of improving your environment," he added. "We believe you want to make a contribution. And we believe you can be trusted."

Many faces around the room were still guarded, but some people were leaning forward, hanging on his words. And, guarded or not, he had absolutely everyone's attention.

"These aren't just a set of empty ideas," Tom said, turning his back to the board. "We want to build them into the foundation of the way we do business at MedTec. Or maybe, I should say, the way we play the game. We don't want you to be cogs in a big machine. We want you to have a say in what happens around here. Especially in your own areas, and about your own jobs. Because you're the expert there. We aren't. Your boss isn't. The only reason for us to tell you how to do what needs to get done would be if we didn't think you could learn, or we didn't think you could be trusted. But that's not true. We think you're unique individuals, creative, capable of learning, capable of making good decisions. And we want to put you in a position to use your abilities. We want to put you in the game.

"As most of you know, we had an explosion on the manufacturing floor last week that could have been prevented if we'd just trusted the tech on duty to follow his own instincts. A lot of you have put in a lot of extra effort to help us recover from that incident. But we could have saved all that effort just by freeing him to do what he knew was right. That's what we want to do here at MedTec: give each of you the freedom to make the decisions you know are best, both for you and the company."

A hand went up at one of the tables. Tom called on a middle-aged man in a researcher's lab jacket, with a smart-guy smirk. "What if what's good for me isn't good for the company?"

Around the room, a few people dared low laughter.

"Great question," Tom said. "At least I can see you're listening. It's good for you to have a job, right?"

The guy nodded.

"You like this one?"

The guy shrugged. "Depends on the day," he said.

"Fair enough," Tom told him. "And I'm sure on some days you'd rather stay in bed than come in. Or you'd rather spend your budget on a trip to Mexico than on the supplies you need."

The guy nodded again, to show Tom had understood his drift.

"That's the way a kid thinks," Tom said. "But we don't

think you're kids here. We think you're adults, capable of making good decisions. Ones that are good for the company, and good for you, because you're part of the company. So we believe you're capable of deciding to spend your budget on things that benefit the company. Because when the company benefits, you benefit. And you're not just here for a paycheck," Tom went on.

"I'm not?" the guy said.

"I am," someone called from the back.

Tom shook his head. "That's part of it," he said. "An important part. And we want to keep the company healthy so you can keep getting paid. But money's not our purpose."

Out of the corner of his eye, he could see Jim shift uncomfortably.

"This company doesn't exist so people can give us money and we can take it," Tom said. "It exists because people out there are sick or hurt, and they need the devices we make. That's why any company exists: because people need shoes, or food, or books, or information. That's why you and I come to work. To provide the world with one of those things. You're doing something that's meaningful, every day. You're doing something that matters. In fact, what you're doing here at MedTec, for some of our customers, is literally a matter of life and death.

"If you're being treated like a kid, it's easy to forget that. Easy to just show up and take the paycheck. But that's not what we're about here. We want you to be a part of making something that matters. Because people are depending on us. Families are depending on us. And we want you to make

43

real decisions about how the things we make for them here get made."

Another hand went up, this time a woman with curly red hair. Despite her striking cat-eye glasses, her voice was shy. "I'm sorry," she said. "I'm just not really sure how all this is going to work. I understand about making decisions for your area. That makes a lot of sense. But it's not always one man standing in front of one machine. A lot of decisions have a lot of moving pieces to them. If all of us are supposed to make decisions now, who decides who gets to make them?"

"We arm wrestle," a joker called from the back of the room.

Tom nodded. "Great," he said. "Another good question. We don't want leaders making all the decisions at MedTec. But they will make one very important set of decisions: they'll identify the decision maker in their area, on different decisions and projects."

"But then whose fault will it be?" the woman asked. "If something goes wrong?"

Tom heard in her question the strong echo of Harkness's blame-based management. He forced a smile. "First of all, we believe you're going to make good decisions," he said. "Just as good or better than the ones we might make. But everyone will be responsible for their own decisions. If you make a bad call, that's on you. If there's no consequence to the decisions you make, there's not really much of a decision there. It's just like having the ball in a game. When you've got it, you might make the shot, or you might blow it. That's true for anyone who's got the ball, coach or players. What we think here at MedTec is that the coaches need to take fewer shots, and let our team members spend more time playing. But the players are still responsible for the shots they take. If you miss too many, you'll hear about it. And the coaches are responsible, too. They'll be responsible for the choices they make about who they put in the game, and when."

The woman looked worried.

"Otherwise, I could talk all day, but this would be nothing more than lip service," Tom told her. "If the person who makes the decision doesn't have any responsibility, the decision doesn't mean anything."

He looked back over the crowd. "Together, over the coming weeks and months, we'll work out what all this means" he said. "I'll be meeting with your leaders, and with you, as we hammer out the details. But I wanted to bring you all together to make this commitment to you as a group. We believe you're unique, creative, trustworthy. Able to make great decisions. And we're going to prove we believe it—by giving decisions to you."

The applause as Tom stepped away from the podium wasn't exactly a standing ovation, but it was a shade less tepid than he'd heard in other business settings. His management team, on the other hand, looked even less enthusiastic now than they had when he started talking.

Tom went over to Jim. "How'd it go?" he asked.

"I'm not sure we'll know that for a while," Jim said.

Around the room, the hum of conversation rose as people stood to go. "—for decisions in our area?" Tom overheard.

"Don't worry about it," came another voice, with a

supervisor's commanding tone. "It's just another one of these business fads. Wait a week. It'll blow over."

Tom spun around, but it was impossible to pick the pair out of the crowd.

When he turned back, Angela, the company's director of human resources, stood beside Jim. Her lips were tight, and she didn't make any effort to hide the displeasure in her eyes.

"Can I talk with you?" she asked.

6.

You're The Expert

"For a leadership team that wants to be all about driving decisions down in the company,," Angela said, "this is one of the most top-down decisions I've ever seen."

The three of them had retreated from the company meeting to Tom's office. Tom sat behind his desk, Angela and Jim in the pair of chairs across from it.

"Look," Angela said, "I can see putting procedures in place so a tech can turn off a threatened machine. That's a no-brainer. And you can't say I haven't heard you out. But I still don't believe that one incident is a reason to upend the management culture of this entire company. Maybe manufacturing needs a bit more leeway to make common-sense decisions. But what about decisions that require expertise and training? Are we going to try to delegate decisions that require advanced degrees in science? What about finance? Strategic planning?"

"I'm sure any strategic plan can benefit from the input of people beyond a small circle of managers," Tom said.

"Hiring and firing," Angela went on. "Insurance. Do you really think these decisions can be handled by the average worker instead of specialists? Do you really think the average worker *wants* to deal with health insurance? Involving other people just sounds like a lot of extra work—for me."

"I'm not sure if the average person would like to deal with insurance or not," Tom said. "But it'd be interesting to find out. It certainly has a big effect on how they live their lives. They might like to drill down into the nitty-gritty, see how those decisions are getting made, weigh the costs themselves, instead of just checking one of three boxes when enrollment time comes around."

"And what value will that add," Angela asked, "beyond a perhaps-immeasurable bump in morale? Teaching someone else the ins and outs of the insurance plans, even for a company this size, is a giant make-work project."

"Perhaps," Tom said. "But at the end of it, you've got more than one person in the company who understands the insurance plans. The company's in better shape, because we've still got that knowledge if the one guy who understood insurance leaves for some reason. And multiple perspectives are always good. You never know what kind of savings or innovations can come out of having another set of eyes on a problem."

Angela was upset, but she wasn't unreasonable. She nodded, giving him the point. "It's just so extreme," she said. "All this upheaval, over one single event."

"It's not just that event," Tom told her. Briefly, he described the conversations he'd had and overheard the day after the machine exploded: Ben's unwillingness to give Anton the freedom to make decisions. Anton's hesitance to take on more decisions, even at Tom's insistence. The deep cynicism of the pinball players in the lounge. "We don't want this to be another business where people check their minds at the door," he told her. "We want them engaged when they're here. Right now, they're not."

"And you think changing the way decisions are made in the company will change all that?" Angela asked.

"I think the way decisions are made tells you more about an organization than anything else it does," Tom said. "It's the quality of decisions that determine the success or failure of any organization. I think people are most creative and motivated to make good decisions when they've got real control. And real responsibility."

Angela's brows drew together as she considered this. "I don't know," she said finally, shaking her head. "I have to tell you, I'm not sure it's a safe bet to try a shakeup of this magnitude, especially with the recent change in ownership."

"Tell you what," Tom said. "You've brought up a whole host of good questions. You're the expert in your area. You know more than I do about how these ideas will work. I want you to be the decision-maker on implementing these changes throughout the human resources department. I'll remind the other leaders to let the whole company know this is a top priority for us. You've got the responsibility, but you've also got the freedom. Think through these questions.

Figure out what you think will work best. Do whatever you need to. If you want to connect with other people who are thinking about this, get advice from other businesses, you let me know. Whatever research you need to do, we'll make it happen. And then come to me with your decisions about how to handle human resources going forward."

"So you can sign off on them?" Angela challenged.

Tom shook his head. "Nope," he said. "So I understand what's happening in the business."

Angela took a deep breath. "All right," she said. "I'll do my best."

"That's exactly what we're looking for," Tom said.

Angela rose to go. At the door, she stopped and turned back. "Thanks," she said.

Tom nodded. The door closed behind her.

Tom took a deep breath, and looked at Jim. "You added a lot to that conversation," he said.

Jim raised his eyebrows. "I used up all my conversation trying to explain these ideas of yours to Helen Harris," he said. "She says they sound crazy enough that we should have disclosed them as risk factors when we met with her about making an investment."

Tom laughed. Helen had a sharp sense of humor.

"I told her I didn't know this was going to be our strategy when we took her money," Jim went on. "You only just came up with it last week."

"What'd she say?" Tom asked.

Jim got to his feet. "She says she invested in us as a team," he says. "And for now, she's willing to trust the team."

"Great," Tom said.

"But she's going to want to be a little more hands-on than she otherwise would," Jim added. "Weekly calls. Regular finance reports."

"Understandable."

Jim nodded in a way that suggested Helen's forbearance went way beyond the understandable. "She's willing to let it play out," Jim said. Then he held up his clipboard in a gesture of warning: "Just as long as the numbers stay strong."

7.

It's All Up To You

Vanessa looked worried. "Okay," she said, in a tone of voice that suggested it was anything but.

"Great," Tom said. He could see she wasn't totally comfortable with the idea, but nobody embraced new ideas, not at first. And even if people were slightly uncomfortable with change, MedTec needed it. That much was clear.

"Okay," he said. "I'm just going to give you a few parameters, and other than that, you can set my schedule any way you think is best. Sophia and I have agreed that the family does better if I don't travel more than three days at a time. When I'm in the office, I want to be home by six, unless there's a very good reason for it. Lunch reservations, you can do your worst, but unless the person I'm meeting with insists, I'm not crazy about Thai food." He leaned back in his chair. "That's pretty much it," he said. "Other than that, it's all up to you."

He had seen her jot down everything he said, but she still watched him, expectant. When he didn't add anything, she shifted in her seat. "Is there anything else?" she said. She glanced down at the brief list in front of her. "Are there any … airlines you prefer?"

Tom shook his head. "That's all up to you," he said. "I'll trust you to decide."

Vanessa glanced down unhappily.

Tom started to feel frustrated. "Vanessa," he said. "I'm sure you can do this. And this isn't really such a big step. I understand Harkness wanted you to check in with him on everything, but admins set schedules for executives all the time. I don't think I've ever made an actual plan with my buddy Sam. You try to talk with him about his schedule and his eyes glaze over. He just tells you to call up Julie, his admin. And then he does whatever she tells him."

"I know," Vanessa said. She gave him a weak smile, obviously trying to put a good face on it.

"But…?" Tom prompted.

Vanessa pursed her lips for a moment, searching for words. "I just want to do a good job," she said finally.

"I'm sure you will."

Vanessa looked down again at the list in her lap. "I've set schedules before," she said. "It's not that. It's just—I'm not exactly sure what you want."

Tom thought back to his speech about the basketball game. He had talked about how not everyone felt comfortable with the ball in their hands. It looked like that was true of Vanessa. He was sure she could do the work. That didn't seem to be the problem. She just didn't like the idea of taking on risk—probably because she'd learned from experience that it was best to avoid it.

"I'm not sure either," Tom said. "That's the whole point. Neither of us really knows what the year will bring. I couldn't possibly give you a set of rules detailed enough to cover everything, even if I wanted to. But you're a very smart woman. I believe you'll make the right call, whatever situations come up."

"But what if I don't?" Vanessa said, her voice rising with worry. "You don't understand, Mr. Anderson. I need this job. I took it to make a little extra three years ago, and thank God I did, because last year Juan got hurt and now he can't work. This is all we've got. I don't want to lose it. I'm a good admin. Mr. Harkness told me what he wanted, and I did it. Whatever he said. I don't need all these choices. You just tell me what you want. I'll do it."

"What I want," Tom said, "is for you to make these decisions. But listen. I'm not saying when you walk out the door today, you can't ever ask me another question. I trust you to make these decisions. But if you want my input, on anything at all, I'm here."

For the first time, Vanessa's expression began to relax. "Okay," she said, and offered him the first real smile she'd given him since he'd asked her to take over the schedule. "I might have a lot of questions."

"That's absolutely fine," Tom said. "But I suspect you'll pick things up so fast that you won't wind up with nearly as many as you thought."

Vanessa's smile widened. "Maybe," she said.

"Listen," Tom said, "it might be scary for me, too. I mean, who knows what kinds of restaurants I'm going to wind up at if I put myself in your hands?"

Vanessa laughed at his joke.

"I know you don't expect to be happy at work," Tom told her.

Vanessa opened her mouth to protest, but he went on. "But you're here eight, nine hours a day. That's most of your waking life. You're not a machine. You've got ideas and opinions. You see things nobody else sees. I don't want you to check that at the door. I want all those ideas and thoughts of yours to work for MedTec."

He could see curiosity and something that might even be hope begin to light up in Vanessa's eyes.

"Why do you come to work every day?" he asked her.

"So I can take care of my family," she answered promptly.

Tom nodded. "Okay," he said. "That's a good reason. It's great that this job lets you take care of your family. And maybe there isn't anything more important to you in the world. But we didn't hire you so that you can take care of your family. We hired you for the way you can help MedTec fulfill its purpose."

Vanessa repeated the comments Tom had made at the company meeting. "To make devices," she said. "To help people. To save lives."

"Exactly," Tom said. "And that's what I want you to do every day when you come in. Not follow orders. I want you to use your unique creativity to help us change people's lives."

Vanessa nodded slowly. "All right," she said. "I'll try."

"That's all we're asking," Tom said. "We'll start small. Just my schedule. And then we'll see where it goes from there."

Vanessa picked up the notebook from her lap. "As many questions as I want?" she said.

"Try me," Tom said.

"I will," Vanessa promised, and went out.

As the door closed behind her, Tom leaned back at his desk. It was almost mind-boggling to think that Vanessa had spent decades of her professional life following orders like a cog in the machine. He wondered how much had been lost because nobody ever listened to her or gave her a chance to make her own decisions. How much waste had gone unnoticed? How many opportunities had been missed?

He was going to try to find out. And if it meant having more conversations like this one, or even having them over and over again, that was all right with him.

In the meantime, though, he was glad for a short break in his schedule. Jim had sent him several documents to review, and Tom had been meaning to get to them for a while. With a sigh of satisfaction, Tom pulled up his email and clicked on the first document to open it. As it flashed up on the screen, the door to his office swung open again. It was Vanessa.

"I have someone here to see you," she said. "Ben Malkmus, from manufacturing."

Tom glanced at the document on his screen. "Does he need to see me right now?" he said.

Vanessa raised her eyebrows, clearly intending to remind him of the eloquent speeches he'd just made about giving her control of his schedule. "I think it's important," she said.

Tom nodded in a gesture of surrender, and clicked a button to shrink the document on his screen.

"Send him on in," he said.

8.

The Ugly Ditch

"Ben," Tom said. "Great to see you. Please, have a seat." Ben settled into one of the chairs opposite Tom's desk. Tom took his own seat again. "What can I do for you?"

"I thought it'd be good to talk," Ben said, "about some of these new ideas you're rolling out."

His expression wasn't worried like Vanessa's had been, but he didn't look exactly happy, either.

Tom settled into his chair and braced himself.

"Nobody's more on board with all this than me," Ben told him. "It's all great. Creativity. Common sense. I get it."

Tom nodded. "Great. So how have you been working those ideas out on the floor?"

"Well," Ben said. "I've got to tell you, sometimes there's an ugly ditch between what you'd like to see happen and what does."

"What are you seeing?" Tom asked.

"Honestly, I'm not really sure the people we've got here in manufacturing are cut out for this kind of thinking," Ben told him. "I mean, give a tech the power to turn off a machine that's about to blow, sure. I'm not going to argue with that. It happened on my floor. And as far as the rest of it goes, like I said, I'm on board. I'm just not sure they are."

"What do you mean?" Tom asked.

"You heard Anton when you came down there, even before the meeting," Ben said. "People who take these line jobs lead a bit more of a punch-the-clock, buy-a-beer life. You've got guys over there in the design labs who might be motivated to be creative. These guys on the manufacturing floor, they just want to get the job done and go home."

"Tell me about some of places you've encouraged people to make decisions," Tom said. "How has it gone?"

Ben shifted in his chair. "Well," he said. "We changed that policy about managerial permissions for line shutdowns, for one thing. Changed that the same day as your meeting. Whoever's supervising any machinery is now authorized to shut down a distressed machine at their own discretion. That's been a weakness in the procedures for a long time. We should have changed it years ago."

Tom nodded. "And how has that been working?"

Ben shrugged. "To tell the truth, that thing with Anton might have been a once-in-a-lifetime. The machines don't go down like that very often. That's why we got by for so long with the old procedure."

"Absolutely," Tom said. "Tell me about how other changes have been working."

"That's the thing," Ben said. "The shop's running great. We've got the problem with the shutdown permissions ironed out. Everyone already knows what they need to do. I don't think there's much else to it."

"So who's making most of the decisions in the shop?" Tom asked.

"There aren't that many to make," Ben said. "The place kind of runs itself, you know?"

"Sure," Tom said. "But if something goes wrong. Or something needs to be changed. Who makes the decision?"

"I guess I do," Ben said after a minute.

"I'd like to see you pass some of those decisions on," Tom said.

Ben leaned forward. "Tom," he said. "These aren't the college-educated guys you've got over in research. These are line workers."

"I understand that," Tom said. "But it doesn't matter whether you have a degree or not. Nobody knows more about how to do your job than you do."

"But it's not their job to make decisions when something goes wrong. Or to set strategy for the shop," Ben said.

"Why not?" Tom asked. "You think you're smarter than every other person on the floor?"

Ben held his hands up. "Hold on," he said. "I wasn't saying that. It's just that I've got years of experience, as a manager—"

"And they've got years of experience," Tom broke in, "actually doing the work. How about scheduling shifts? Who does that now?"

"I do," Ben said.

"That's something you could hand off to someone else on the floor," Tom said.

"I'm not sure everybody down there could do that," Ben said. "It gets pretty complicated. You have to watch over-time. You've only got a set amount for payroll. And then there are vacations to work around. People get sick and have emergencies."

"That's where you make your choice as a leader," Tom said. "You don't close your eyes and point. You pick someone you know is up to it. Someone you think will do a great job."

"I'm not sure they'd want to if I did," Ben said. "It's a lot of extra work for them."

"Why don't you choose someone and ask them," Tom said. "You might be surprised."

"You're the boss," Ben said, his mouth tightening.

"How about workflow?" Tom asked. "You think the peo-ple on the line might see efficiencies or waste no one else does?"

"I keep a pretty close eye on that kind of thing," Ben said.

"Why don't you choose someone you think can handle it," Tom said. "And have them do their own analysis?"

"Okay," Ben said. He was doing his best to sound agree-able, but he didn't meet Tom's eyes. "And then we can decide what to do about it."

"Nope," Tom said. "It's their decision. That's the whole idea here. We don't want to make a lot of extra work for people, when we don't give them any power. It's not a shell game. We want to give them real decisions to make. Ones that affect their workplace. Ones that mean something. Environmental compliance. That's another area you could bring someone else into. Innovation. Your people must have ideas about how things could work better. Let's have them lead some projects, put them into action."

"But what if they make a bad decision?" Ben objected.

"Have you ever made a bad decision?" Tom asked.

Ben studied Tom's face. "Everybody has," he said, his tone slightly defensive.

"I have, too," Tom said. "Probably more bad ones than you have. Just because you've got 'manager' somewhere in your title doesn't mean you're immune from making bad decisions. And not being a manager doesn't mean you can't make good ones."

"I never said that," Ben said.

"Well, let's give someone else a chance to make decisions, too, then," Tom said. "How about supplies? You do that, too?"

Ben nodded. "They let me know what they need, and I order every two weeks."

"What if everyone ordered for their own station?" Tom asked. "Think that might cut out any waste?"

"It's not that simple," Ben said. "These devices are complicated. They might have dozens of different parts."

"But each person knows what they need to get their job done," Tom said. "Don't they?"

Ben nodded, reluctantly. "It's just if they forget, the whole line—"

"Have you ever forgotten to place an order?" Tom asked.

Ben, still reluctant, nodded again.

"My guess is, you'll be less likely to forget an order if you know you've got to have the supplies to do your job," Tom said. "And if the decision's really yours. And you don't have your boss to fall back on."

Ben gave a slight shrug. "I guess so," he said.

"It sounds to me like you've got some good decisions you can release on the manufacturing side," Tom said. "I'd love to hear about it when you think of more."

Ben nodded, although the gesture seemed more automatic than enthusiastic. "You want me to run them by you?" he asked. "See what you think about them?"

"I'm glad to talk through them with you," Tom said. "Any time. But if you've got something you want to try in your own area, you don't need my say-so. That's your decision."

9.

What About Them?

"They're great ideas," Mike said. "Brilliant, really. In fact—" He leaned back in his desk chair and smiled with the air of a guy who was used to being called brilliant himself. "—we already had a lot of them in place here in R&D."

Tom watched his head of R&D, who was seated in front of towering bookshelves stuffed with scientific books and journals, and littered with papers and tiny pieces of machinery. In the weeks since the company meeting, Tom had met with various team leaders to work on ways to give their people more decisions. But Mike's reaction was by far the most positive he'd heard yet.

"Yeah?" Tom said. "Tell me about that."

Mike spread his hands as if the points were so obvious they hardly bore repeating. "Well, you can hardly tell a top-level researcher how to do their job," he said. "By definition, they're striking out into new territory. If you already knew how to tell them to get where they're going, you wouldn't need them to do the research in the first place.

"Not to mention," Mike added, "most researchers don't have a personality that takes well to babysitting from management. Even if you could give them a checklist, they wouldn't follow it. That's not how they're built. It's what makes them good researchers. So I've always given my people a lot of freedom. In research, it's just common sense."

Tom nodded.

"But try telling that to Harkness," Mike said. "That guy wanted reports. He wanted benchmarks—on research. Those two words don't even make sense together in a sentence. You wouldn't believe how much time I wasted, reporting on measurements that didn't have any bearing at all on whether or not we were doing good research. And, of course, I'd never get anything out of my people if I tried to make them do what Harkness thought he wanted.

"But you're right," he said, grinning at Tom. "I'm the expert in how to do my job. I don't need someone else telling me what to do. Not on my own turf. It feels great to have a boss who finally recognizes that."

"What about your lab techs?" Tom asked.

Mike looked surprised. "The techs?" he said. "What about them?"

"More than two thirds of your staff on the R&D side don't have researcher positions. How do all these ideas work out for them?"

Mike shrugged. "Ah, you know," he said. "The support jobs aren't the same as the research positions. Researchers, they've got to be creative. It's a job requirement. With the techs—" he hesitated, thinking how to put it. "The expectations are, shall we say, clear. The jobs are about execution and precision. You don't want a tech getting creative with your specs. You want your specs followed perfectly, down to the millimeter."

"Sure," Tom said. "But they still have decisions to make. Priorities. Workflow. Even the choices they make in how they execute your specs."

"I guess so," Mike said, dubious but willing to be agreeable. Then he brightened. "They do great, though," he said. "Just what we tell them to. We never have any problem in that area."

"You know," Tom said, "I'd love to talk with a couple of your researchers and techs. See if they've got anything else they'd add to the mix."

"Sure, absolutely," Mike said immediately, and rose from behind his desk.

The feel of the R&D labs was almost the opposite of the vibe on the manufacturing floor. The manufacturing floor was dwarfed by tall ceilings, dimly lit with fluorescent bulbs. It was so noisy you had to raise your voice to be heard over the wail and shriek of the machines. In contrast, the R&D labs were quiet, clean, and flooded with natural light from large windows. Most of the researchers sat at computers in glassed-in offices. At a large workshop in the center of the complex, a group of techs worked on prototypes, modeling components with sophisticated software or fabricating samples.

Mike led Tom to one of the nearby offices, knocked on the door, and stuck his head in. "Jane," he said. "I've got Tom Anderson here. You have a minute?"

A pleasant-faced woman, middle-aged, with brown hair in straight blunt cut, looked up from a thick hardcover book that lay open on her desk and smiled. "Tom," she said. "Good to see you. I really appreciated your comments the other day."

"Glad to hear it," Tom said.

"Tom's interested in how those ideas are working out here in R&D," Mike told her.

"Oh," Jane said. "Mike's great. We've always had the autonomy we need to do good work here. He stays out of our way."

"I know a good thing when I see it," Mike said.

Jane beamed.

"So who are you working with on your current projects?" Tom asked.

Jane looked confused.

"Which techs?" Tom clarified. "You've got people on modeling and fabrication, right?"

"Oh," Jane said. "Sure. Let me just..." She turned to her computer, clicked through a few screens, and read from the upper corner of a document. "Simmons," she said. "And Vasquez."

"I'd love to talk with them," Tom said. "Would you like to come with us?"

Jane stood. "I'm always up for a field trip," she said.

"Vasquez," Mike said, when they reached the shop area.

By the way he scanned the room, Tom could tell he didn't know exactly who he was looking for.

A young man who had been frowning in concentration at a 3-D image in a modeling program looked up.

"Simmons," Mike added. A woman who stood over a small machine that made a low hum and an even series of convincing thunks looked up.

Mike gestured for them to come over. "We've got Tom Anderson here," he said. "He wants to talk with us about the new ideas he mentioned at the meeting last week. I told him there wasn't much for you to do in the way of decision-making. Mostly following directions in your positions, I know. But he'd like to talk with you anyway."

Simmons and Vasquez looked at Tom, silent.

"I know researchers already have a lot of freedom in R&D," Tom said. "I'm curious about your positions, if you see any room for improvement."

Simmons gave a game smile. "Oh, we're just following orders, mostly," she said. "That's the job. Just getting the job done."

Tom nodded and moved toward the work station she had just left. "And what are you doing over here?" he asked.

"Just fabricating a prototype," she said. "Jane sent us the specs this morning. Vasquez tweaked the model, and now I'm keeping an eye on the build. This machine works by addition, instead of subtraction. We don't carve anything out of the material. Instead, we're building it up based on the computer model, layer by layer. This one's for the smaller pieces. We've got a bigger one over there," she said, pointing.

"You say Vasquez tweaked the model," Tom said. He turned to the young man. "What does that mean?"

The tech looked guarded. "I just cleaned a few things up," he said.

"What kind of things?" Tom asked.

Vasquez glanced at Jane, then at Mike, then back at Tom. "Sometimes the models don't really work in the real world," he said. "You just need to fix them so they do."

"You did that here?" Tom asked.

Vasquez nodded.

"We adjusted the material," Simmons added. "Sometimes they ask for one thing, but you know it won't work. It's no problem. You just find something that does."

"And this morning—?" Tom began.

Simmons nodded.

"What was wrong with the material I ordered?" Jane broke in, her voice curious rather than annoyed. "It should have had more than enough flexibility for the application."

"That was the problem," Simmons told her. "It was too flexible to support the other parts we've been modeling. It would have compromised the whole design. So I chose something I knew would work better with all the other components of the device."

"That'd be good to know," Jane said. "It could help me when I move on to the next parts."

Simmons looked surprised. "Oh, sure," she said. "I just didn't want to bother you. I didn't think it was important."

"That's the thing about research," Jane said. "You never know what's important."

"So what kinds of decisions would you make?" Tom asked, turning back to the two techs. "If you were in charge of the workshop?"

The question struck Vasquez and Simmons silent again. Simmons glanced at Mike.

"I can see everything's working well the way it is," Tom said, to smooth the waters. "You've got a good lab here. But what about bright ideas? Anything you could make work better?"

"Well," Vasquez said after a minute, "I spend a lot of time fixing the models that come down from research."

"Are that many of them wrong?" Jane said.

Vasquez nodded. "A lot of them are," he said. "I don't mind the work. But we could get more done in a day if the models were right when they came in. And you could get your parts back faster."

"I had no idea you were spending so much time fixing our models," she said. "I just send them down to you, and the parts come back up."

"Why haven't you told anyone this?" Mike asked.

"Researchers don't really like it when you tell them what to do," Vasquez observed. Simmons suppressed a smile. "Especially not if you're a tech."

Mike frowned. "These decisions affect productivity," he said.

"It sounds like the techs are doing more than just following directions," Tom agreed.

The nearby machine let out an especially vigorous thunk. A light on the top came on, along with a high warning tone.

Simmons turned back, dismayed. "Excuse me," she said. "I need to take a look at this. Do you mind?"

"Thank you," Tom said. "This has been very helpful."

As Vasquez and Simmons bent over the fabrication machine, Tom, Jane, and Mike trailed back to the researcher offices.

Jane shook her head as they walked. "I feel like we've been treating our techs like robots," she said. "I really appreciate what you're trying to do here."

"Those aren't the only changes I'm interested in," Tom said as they reached her office. "On the manufacturing side, Ben's going to start having some of his people take responsibility for workflow, scheduling, supplies. I'd like to see researchers start to take on similar responsibilities."

"I don't know," Jane said as she took her seat at her desk. "I'm a research nerd, always have been. I really just want to run my numbers and be left alone. That, and a bigger budget." She grinned.

"If you took on some of the responsibility for budget planning," Tom said, "you might understand more of what Mike's dealing with when he sets a budget for you. Or be in a better position to make your pitch."

Jane raised her eyebrows. "Maybe," she said.

Mike's face was troubled when he and Tom stepped out of Jane's office, back into the hall. "That's a big problem you just turned up," he said. "Why wouldn't the workshop bring something that big to me?"

"It sounds like no one ever asked them before," Tom said.

"I guess not," Mike said. "But with my researchers, I never

have to ask. If they get a hangnail, I never hear the end of it."

"All you wanted the techs to do was follow directions," Tom said. "That's what they were trying to do."

"They're making a lot of decisions on their own," Mike said.

"That's the thing about people," Tom said. "Even when we try to treat them like robots, they can't stop being creative. We can't shut it off, even if we wanted to. And we don't. It's a good thing, not a problem."

Mike raised his eyebrows, doubtful. "You sure about that?" he asked.

10.

Watch The Numbers

"They look good," Tom said.

Jim sat in one of the chairs across from Tom's desk, gazing down at a copy of the monthly report.

"We're still short of our projections," Jim pointed out.

"That's because of the explosion," Tom said. "Not the new strategies. We're actually ahead of where we expected to be when we ran the projections based on the shut-down in manufacturing."

"I can see that," Jim said.

"We've gained ground using the new system," Tom insisted.

"It's still early in the game," Jim told him.

"Yes," Tom allowed. "But, for instance, did you look at sales? Sales are up. And that's not just a bump from normal fluctuations. That's a significant amount."

Jim nodded cautiously.

"I've talked to a few of our salespeople," Tom said, "asking for an explanation. It's the decision-making. Harkness had them calling managers to sign off on any deal they negotiated. It could take hours to get review and approval, and over a certain amount, Harkness wanted to look at it himself. That gave customers a lot of time to cool down, renegotiate—or change their mind. Now they're free to make a deal themselves. And it's created a significant bump in sales."

"If they've been making good deals," Jim said.

"Well, with the deals they were making before, the company was sinking toward the red," Tom said. "Right now we've got a volume increase. I'll ask them to look into it, give us an analysis of how these deals compare to the ones they were making under Harkness."

"I'd like to see that," Jim said.

"We've got a slight dip in personal expenses on the sales team, too," Tom said.

"Where'd that came from?"

"They took the limits off the expense accounts."

"And that made the expenses go down?"

"Yep," Tom said. "Because they also told each salesperson how much had been allotted to them in this year's budget for expenses. And that if anything was left over, they could spend it at their own discretion to build the business."

"Interesting," Jim said.

"Vanessa's even getting on board with the decision-making," Tom said, and grinned. "She sent me to a Mediterranean place yesterday. Nice change from the national chain restaurants."

Jim didn't return his smile.

"Hey," Tom said. "What's wrong? These numbers look good. Better than we expected."

"I know they're good," Jim said. "It just doesn't feel good."

"What do you mean?"

Jim shook his head. "It's hard to say," he said. "You're right, the sales look great.

"But I used to know that you were on top of things. You had it all under control. You spent your time looking at the big picture. And now you're spending all your time giving these decisions to someone else. I guess I'm just not convinced they're going to be making the same caliber of decisions you would. I know the numbers look good this month. But I wonder what they're going to look like down the road, long term."

"This new strategy *is* my decision," Tom said. "I've thought about it just as much as I've thought about all the other decisions I've ever made. You trusted me on those. You can trust me on this. I believe our people can make decisions just as good as mine. Maybe better. And I think we'll be a better company if we let them.

"I can't tell you what's going to happen down the road," he continued. "Nobody can. But I'm sure we're going in the right direction. And the numbers are good this month. I don't know what else we could ask."

"I don't either," Jim said. "Or I'd ask it." He let the cover of the folder that held the monthly report fall closed. "But I don't want you to think I'm sold on this yet. As far as I'm concerned, we're still testing this out. And returning to business as usual isn't out of the question."

Tom nodded. "What did Helen say?" he asked.

"She still doesn't understand exactly what we're doing here," Jim said. "And I'm not sure I did a great job of explaining it to her, because I'm not sure I do either. But she understood the numbers. They look good to her. She's happy as long as they're moving in a positive direction."

Tom nodded. "Good," he said. He closed his own folder.

"Thank you," he added. "I know what we're doing here isn't traditional. But it's tapping into cutting-edge business thinking. People are motivated by real control, real responsibility. And it's common sense. Layers of bureaucracy only slow us down and take the decisions further away from the people who really know what's happening. You'll see. As we choose decision-makers and give them real responsibility, the business will only get stronger. But I understand the concern. And I appreciate your trust."

"I trust you," Jim said. "But I trust the numbers most of all. And if they start to turn south, I don't know if I can let it go on. I'm not going to let this business run aground as a favor to a friend."

"That's fair," Tom said. He glanced at the clock on the wall. "Angela will be coming in in a few minutes. Do we have anything else?"

For the first time, Jim gave a wry smile. "Besides my concerns about the overarching strategy for the business and its long-term health?" he said. "I don't think so, nope."

Tom grinned as he rose. "I hear you," he said. "And I think you'll see."

The intercom button lit up on Tom's phone. He pressed

it to listen. "I have Angela here to see you," Vanessa announced.

11.

If You're Serious

"Angela," Tom said, and shook her hand. She turned to take Jim's hand as well, then sat down beside him, across from Tom's desk.

"Thanks so much for coming," Jim said.

Tom and Jim took their seats again. Angela shuffled a sheaf of notes on her lap.

"It looks like you've got a few thoughts there," Jim said.

"I have more than a few," Angela said.

Tom leaned back in his chair. "Well, great," he said. "Tell us about them."

Angela took a deep breath. "You mentioned some underlying principles during the open meeting," she said. "People are unique. People are creative."

Tom nodded. It sounded like she had absorbed what he'd said, despite her objections. "Yes."

"Well, I've spent quite a bit of time talking with people

in our different areas, about how human resources might integrate those principles," she said. "And I've come up with several more of my own."

Tom bristled. He'd asked her to implement his ideas, not expand on them. She led human resources, not the whole company. Where did she think she got off, setting executive policy? But then he shrugged it off. This was exactly what he'd asked his people to do, he realized. Take ownership of their areas and start making decisions for themselves. Angela just seemed to have done it more thoroughly than anyone else had so far.

To set her at ease, he nodded. "Like what?" he said.

Angela glanced down at her notes. "I call the first one fairness," she said, looking at Jim. "It flows from Tom's point that people are unique. Until now, we've tried to make everything equal on HR issues. Everyone gets the same vacation and sick days. Everyone works through the same structure of seniority and raises."

"Pretty typical," Jim said.

Angela nodded. "Yes," she said. "But when I started playing with the idea that people are unique, I realized that it's not really fair."

"No?" Tom said.

Angela shook her head. "Fairness doesn't mean that everyone should be treated exactly the same," she said. "Right now, we reward people with raises. But people come into my office at least a few times a year who really just want more vacation. They'd rather have that than a bump in pay. Under our current structure, there's nothing I can do for them.

But if I'm authorized to give rewards based on the individual rather than the protocol, I could give them longer vacations, which would make them happier—and save us money."

"That could work," Jim said, somewhat cautiously.

"Same with maternity leave," Angela said. "Some of our people take advantage of it. Some of them never will. It doesn't make sense to try to treat them with perfect equality there, because their experiences are unique."

"Interesting," Tom said.

"Right now, we treat everyone as if they must have exactly the same skills and drive, as long as they've got the same title. They don't," Angela said. "That plays out in two ways. First of all, we pay everyone with the same seniority at basically the same scale, regardless of what they produce. We don't reward people who are working harder. And we over-reward people who aren't.

"But the second way is worse. We pretend everyone has the same strengths and weaknesses. We've got great mechanics who are struggling to sift through piles of paperwork, and people who really love to deal with details who are struggling with mechanics. We promote our researchers into management, when leading people is the last thing they want to do. We haven't placed our people to play to their strengths. So they're wasting a lot of time trying to compensate for their weaknesses.

"If you're serious about these decision-making ideas," she said. "It may affect the job description and compensation of everyone in the organization."

Jim looked at Tom and raised his eyebrows. For once, Tom

shared his obvious skepticism. Angela's claim sounded extreme, even to Tom. He and Jim had wanted to create a good place to work, sure. But rewriting more than two hundred job descriptions and compensation packages was a far cry from installing a pinball machine in the lounge.

Still, he couldn't argue with Angela's logic. And, as he listened to her, possibilities he hadn't even dreamed of began to open up in his mind: job descriptions that were tailored to release the individual strengths of the person who held the position. Compensation that took into account whatever actually motivated each person the most. Angela's suggestions made so much sense that the real question was: why had they ever been doing anything else?

"I see what you're saying," he said.

Jim shifted beside Angela in his chair, with an expression that clearly said, *I'm not sure I do.*

"I have a few more," Angela told them.

Tom tilted his head to indicate she should go on.

"Our organizational chart," she said. "Right now it's broken into silos. I think you're right that our accountants are the experts on accounting."

"So we agree on that," Jim said.

Angela glanced at him, not sure whether to take this as a joke. Tom wasn't sure Jim knew himself. But Angela plunged on. "But our accountants make decisions that affect research and manufacturing," she said. "And research and manufacturing make all kinds of decisions that affect the bottom line. In the current system, they almost never talk to each other. If we let that continue, and give them more power to make their own decisions, their decisions won't make sense for the organization as a whole. We need to start thinking about cross-functional teams, where enough perspectives are represented, and where people have enough information, to really make good decisions."

"So it's not just job descriptions and compensation," Tom joked. "You think we need to remake our entire organizational chart."

"It depends on whether you're serious about these ideas," Angela told him.

Tom raised his eyebrows, both slightly annoyed and highly impressed by the way she'd taken ownership of the new ideas about how decisions should get made. Maybe this was part of what Sophia had warned him about. It was hard to stay out of the game when you were used to being on the court. But at the same time, he felt a new kind of pride— maybe something like a coach feels when one of his players makes a great shot, he thought.

"Anything else?" he said. Jim raised his eyebrows, indicating he couldn't believe there could be anything else. But Angela didn't seem to be finished.

"One other thing," she said. "Our bonus structure. Right now, only leaders get compensated for high performance. But leaders aren't the only people responsible for success in the organization. They couldn't do anything without the support of a team. And we don't have a structure for rewarding team members. We need to look more closely at who really deserves individual bonuses. And if we're going to disperse decision-making as far as you're suggesting, I'd like to think about a general bonus plan, to reward entire teams for their contributions."

"That's a good idea," Tom said. "Although I'd like to think that getting to make these kinds of decisions will create satisfaction in and of itself."

"A bonus never hurts," Angela said. "And we already give them. I just want to make sure we're really rewarding our people for their unique contributions."

She paused and looked across the desk at Tom.

"Is that it?" he asked.

Angela started. "Well, yes," she said, and then began to backpedal. "For now, I mean. I can certainly do more—"

Tom raised a hand. "You've done more than enough," he said. "And I'm impressed. You aren't just following orders. You're coming up with ideas of your own. That's exactly what we want to see happen here at MedTec. And the ideas you've come up with are excellent."

Angela smiled, visibly relieved.

"So tell us about your thoughts for implementing them," Jim said, a hint of challenge in his voice.

Angela straightened and slid away the page she'd been working from to reveal another page of notes. "Well, it's a lot of work," she said. "But I'd like to begin meeting with each team member in the company, find out what really motivates them, and begin working with them to identify their strengths and weaknesses. The second phase would be formalizing new job descriptions, and introducing more fluidity into compensation packages. I'll also start working on the creation of cross-functional teams. It may take a discovery period to really understand what the best mixes will be, and then I'll need to work out those details with each individual area. I'll also begin conversations about how to restructure our bonus packages, and begin to educate our team members so they understand that they'll now be eligible for those benefits as well."

Jim leaned back in his chair and folded his hands behind his head. "I think you may have just rewritten your own job description as well," he said.

Angela smiled. "I don't mind hard work," she told him. "I never have."

"I can see that," Tom said. "And I appreciate it. But tell me: what decisions are left?"

"I'm sorry?" Angela said, her smile fading.

"What decisions are left?" Tom asked. "You've got a very strong grasp of the uniqueness of our people. And you're right that these ideas should release potential we're not currently tapping. But do you really think all these decisions should be made centrally?

"You're very talented, but it's the people in each area who know best how they want to be compensated, who should be rewarded, when it's appropriate in the life of a team for one of the members to go on vacation. They're the ones who know best what kind of information they need to share with other areas, and what kind of information they need themselves."

"Well," Angela objected. "These are big changes. I'm not sure we want to offload decisions of this magnitude to team members who have never dealt with this kind of responsibility before. Not without the oversight of someone who has some expertise in the area."

"Every person who works here has expertise making decisions that matter," Tom said. "They do it all the time in the rest of their lives. They decide what field to go into, who to marry, where to live, how to budget their own finances. There's nobody alive who doesn't have a lifetime of experience making decisions. We just forget that the instant they walk in the door at work."

"Well, not everybody makes good decisions," Angela pointed out.

"True," Tom said. "And not every executive makes good decisions, either. You've seen that right here at MedTec. And the news is full of stories of executive missteps."

Angela nodded, but her expression was stubborn. "I just think you're going to need somebody," she said, "to keep track of all the moving pieces and make sure everything is working."

"But the point is to give that responsibility to the team members who are closest to the decisions," Tom said. "You've grasped all of these other ideas so clearly. I don't understand why you don't see this piece of it, too. This underlies it all. It's absolutely fundamental to what we're trying to do."

"It's just—" Angela said, and stopped. Her face was unhappy.

"What?" Tom said, more gently.

"I can see it makes sense," Angela admitted. "I just don't see where I fit in. You're talking about giving my job away. If we drive all these human resources functions back down into the teams, what will I have to do? What's going to happen to me?"

Tom leaned forward. "I see," he said.

"I don't mind doing this work," Angela repeated. "I believe in what you want to do here."

"Listen," Tom said. "I want you to stop worrying about whether or not you have a job here. You do. But we can't have you making decisions that belong in the teams. So I'd like you to go back to the drawing board and tell me two things. First, I want to hear what you really think is the best way to implement these ideas within the teams. And then I want you to use all the same hard work and creativity you just showed me, to come up with some answers about what your own job will be."

"What do you think will be left for me to do?" Angela asked. "After we give all these decisions to the teams?"

"I don't know," Tom said, with a glance at Jim. "You tell me."

12.

Fallible

Tom and Jim stood side by side in the atrium of the research wing, looking down at a box of metal and polymer devices that Ben, the head of manufacturing, had just dropped on the floor in front of them.

"What are we looking at?" Tom asked.

Mike, the head of research, stood beside Ben on the other side of the box. A few techs began to turn their heads or drift closer, drawn by the conversation. As they watched, Ben pulled one of the devices free from the rest.

"This," he said.

He exerted a small amount of pressure on the device's polymer wing. The wing snapped neatly off.

"Well," Tom said. "These devices aren't made to be manhandled. If you mistreat something, it's going to break."

"I wasn't mistreating it," Ben said. He picked up an unfamiliar tool and applied it to the polymer wing of a second device. A moment later, the new wing snapped off, and a series of numbers flashed on the digital display of the tool. "That looks more official," he said. "But it's the same thing: the standard tolerance test for that piece. And the pressure we're exerting is exactly where you'd expect it to occur once the device is implanted in a patient."

Tom folded his arms. He glanced at Jim. Mike shifted.

"So where is our problem?" Tom asked. "Do we have a problem in manufacturing? Is it an issue with design?"

"It's the new polymer," Ben said, and glanced significantly at Mike. Mike lifted his chin with an air of defiance, but his eyes were worried.

"I haven't heard anything about a new polymer," Jim said.

"We just started using it the past few days," Ben told him. "Following the new specs for this product. Research sent them down. And placed a big order for it—it's taking up half my storage."

"There's a significant price break for quantity orders," Mike broke in.

"You placed the order?" Jim asked him.

"I've been wanting to try some of the new polymers for years," Mike said. "But Harkness never wanted to change anything. I kept telling him they're lighter, more durable, easier to work with, cheaper. No go. But you've finally freed our hands to do some of the things that have needed to be done around here for a long time. Usually I have to turn the sales guys away when they come in, but when the last one came by, he just had a great product. More versatile, less cost. It's going to show gains on the research side, because we can push it further, and in manufacturing, because it's more versatile. And you'll see it in the bottom line, too. It was a great deal."

"What product is this?" Jim asked.

Mike named it.

Jim shook his head.

"What?" Tom said.

"I've worked with it before," Jim told him. "The company spends twice as much on sales as they do on research. They've got some of the best salespeople in the business. Good enough that we ordered it, too, at our last company. But it didn't hold up in any application. I was just like Mike here. I thought it was going to save us money. But it wound up being a total loss."

A brunette woman among the group of nearby techs nodded. "I was at a company that ordered that stuff, too," she said. "We got so many returns, we had to throw out product by the case."

"How long will it take to switch this back to the original specs?" Tom asked Ben.

"Couple weeks," Ben said. "It'll take at least that long to get a full shipment of the original material. We can probably switch over most of the machines while we're waiting for it."

"And how much of this did we order?" Jim asked Mike.

"A six-month supply," Mike said. He looked a little sick. "It cost half as much as what we had been using."

"So we're looking at three months of supply costs as an outright loss," Jim calculated.

"Are you sure you're following the specs we sent down?"

Mike asked Ben. "Materials don't behave as predicted if the specs aren't strictly followed."

"Right," Ben said. "It's always manufacturing's fault. Even when it's research that orders the bad product."

"Okay, okay," Mike said.

Ben dropped the broken device back in the box. "I better get on the phone," he said, and turned to go. "See how quickly our old company can help us out."

"I wish you'd asked someone," Jim said to Mike. "It sounds like either of us could have saved us all a lot of cost and trouble."

"It was my decision," Mike insisted.

Jim looked at Tom and raised his eyebrows.

When they returned to the executive suite, Jim followed Tom into his office. Off to the side of Tom's desk was the whiteboard where he'd been working out decision-making ideas over the past months. In the upper left corner, he'd made a permanent list of his assumptions about their people:

Unique

Creative

Trustworthy

Capable of Learning

Responsible

Like a Challenge

Desire to Contribute

"I think I've got another one for you," Jim said. He pulled the dry erase marker from the aluminum lip of the board. At the bottom of the list, he scrawled: "*Fallible.*"

13.

Advice

Fallible, Tom wrote at the bottom of the list he'd just scrawled on the whiteboard in the company lounge. When he turned back, the entire staff, assembled again, stared back at him, some with interest, some with familiar blank stares.

"We believe all these things are true," Tom said, pointing to the words he'd listed above it: *Unique, Creative ... Desire to Contribute.*

His finger stopped again at *Fallible*. "But we also have to face the fact that we all make mistakes. Me just as much as you. The most experienced person in the world can't make good decisions if they don't have the information they need. So we're going to add another piece to our decision-making around here."

Advice, he wrote on the board behind him, then turned back to the gathered crowd. "The advice process," he said. "It's pretty simple. When you've got a decision to make, you

91

get advice about it. One source is your leader. The others should have some experience with the decision you're making: they've done it before. They've seen it done. Maybe they're even one of our customers. And we don't just want you to ask people who work in positions above you. If you're a researcher, we want you asking techs. If you're managing manufacturing strategy, we want you to hear from people who are actually on the floor. Oftentimes, they know just as much, if not more, than managers do."

The crowd let out a few murmurs of assent. "I'm absolutely certain of that, because I'm a manager," Tom joked.

"The bigger the decision," he went on, "The more people you ask. If you're making a decision that affects the whole company, you might ask a dozen people, and even think about getting outside input from other places that have already done what you're thinking about.

"From here on out," he said, "we want you to consider this part of your job. Not every decision has to be perfect. But absolutely every decision-maker needs to seek advice. To us, that's even more important than getting it right every single time. But I think we'll get it right a lot more often with this process than we would without it.

"This goes for the whole company," he added. "All the way up to me and Jim. We're going to be seeking advice on the decisions we make, just like we expect you to.

"Decisions are fun to make. Too often we hold onto all of them ourselves. That's supposed to be our job as leaders, knowing what to do. But I think we'll make better decisions by following the advice process, too. The CEOs you see in the papers, because their companies are in collapse—they're the ones who didn't ask for advice. Or, if they did, they didn't listen to it."

He paused and stepped away from the whiteboard. "Any questions?"

Holly, the redhead from research, was seated around one of the rectangular tables a few rows back. She raised her hand.

"Yes," Tom said.

"You said we have to ask our boss for advice," she said.

"That's right." Tom nodded.

"But our boss is our boss," she said. "Won't they just tell us what to do? What if we choose to do something besides what they said?"

"Good question." Tom said. "Here's the short answer: I'm their boss, and I'm telling you, it's your decision."

"But it's still our fault if we choose the wrong thing?" someone asked from the back of the room. "Even if we ask for advice first?"

It took Tom a minute to pick him out of the crowd: a middle-aged man with a mop of curly salt-and-pepper hair, wearing a pair of manufacturing's blue overalls.

"Yep," Tom said. "It's not really your decision if there aren't consequences to it. You're responsible for whatever happens. And your boss is responsible, for choosing you to make the decision. But the worst trouble you'll get into won't be for making a mistake. It'll be for not asking for advice. Like I said, asking for the advice will help keep you out of trouble."

A woman in a researcher's white lab jacket raised her hand on the other side of the room. "But you said the boss is responsible, for choosing who makes the decision. Can you talk more about that?" she said. "We've heard a lot about how we need to give decisions away, but not a lot about how to choose the people to give them to."

"That's a great question," Tom said. "Thank you. What I'd like to do, actually, is hear from all of you. What factors do you think should go into choosing a decision-maker?"

The silence in the room lasted so long that Tom started to wonder how long he could stand there without anyone saying anything.

Then a gray-haired woman in a sweatshirt with a lace collar raised her hand. "They should know what they're doing," she said.

"Okay," Tom said. "Expertise. That's certainly a factor." He wrote the phrase on the whiteboard.

"Yeah," a man in the back pointed out, "but a lot of times it's the people who think they know what they're doing who make the biggest mistakes."

"True," Tom said. "We've all seen that before."

"Well, if we're getting this much advice on a decision," said a blonde woman, "maybe it doesn't matter if we're an expert or not. Because we'll have to talk to the experts before we can decide anything."

"Good," Tom said. "So maybe expertise is a factor, but not the only one. What else might be more important?"

"Someone who can listen," the blonde woman said.

Good listener, Tom wrote on the board. "That'll be

important," he said, "to make the advice process work. The best advice in the world can't help someone who won't take it."

While he was still writing, someone else called out, "Someone who you know already makes good decisions."

"Great," Tom said, and added *History of good decisions* to the list.

"Someone who knows the situation," another man added.

"Yes," Tom said, writing *Close to the situation*. "They're more likely to understand the dynamics, and to have expertise. And, if the decision directly affects them, they've got skin in the game. It isn't abstract anymore. They don't just want to get it right for its own sake. They want to get it right because what happens is going to change their life."

"Anything else?" he asked.

The silence that followed didn't seem uncomfortable anymore. Tom could almost hear the thoughts buzzing in the room. After a few moments, someone said, "That looks like a big order to me already." The crowd broke into appreciative laughter.

"I think it's a good list," Tom said. "And I want you to notice something else about it. Based on these characteristics, would a boss usually be the best decision-maker on most problems? Do they always have the most expertise?"

Around the room, heads shook.

"Nope," Tom agreed. "The boss can't always know the most about every problem. That's why we hire all the different people in an area, because one person can't know it all. How about being a good listener? Is that how you usually think of your boss?"

"No comment," someone muttered, loud enough so everyone could hear. Laughter rippled through the room again.

"My boss listens," a woman piped up.

Tom grinned. "Okay," he said. "Some do, some don't. But being a boss doesn't mean you're automatically good at listening. Some people might say it makes us worse. What about a history of good decisions?"

"That can be hard to tell," a woman pointed out. "In my area, we don't get to make many."

"Fair enough," Tom said. "And hopefully, as we move forward with all this, that's going to change. But the reality is, we see people around us make decisions all the time. Not just at work, but in the rest of their lives. You've got ideas about whether you think those decisions are good or not. What do you think? Are bosses better at making decisions than everyone else?"

Heads began to shake.

Tom pointed at the next item. "Close to the problem," he said. "Are the bosses usually the closest to any given situation?"

"They're the furthest," someone said. "Sometimes you've got two, three people between them and whatever's actually happening."

"And that's just in our company," Tom said. "In bigger organizations, you're talking half a dozen layers. But we'll still take a situation that we're working with every day, or a decision that's going to affect everything we do, and take it to a boss so they can decide. They haven't been there. And if they don't ask anyone else for advice, all they've got to work with is what we tell them. Does that make sense to you?"

A chorus of "no"s rose in the room.

"And anyone in this company, from line worker to researcher, if they've got these qualities—" Tom pointed back at the list "—and if they ask at least four people for advice—people who have done it before, people above them and below them—do you think they're going to be able to make a good decision?"

It took him a minute to realize the sound he heard was clapping. As that fact dawned on him, more and more people joined in, until the room filled with applause. Tom let it go for a few moments, surprised and strangely touched. Then he held up his hands.

"Thank you," he said. "But I don't want you to clap for me. I want you to clap for yourselves. You're the ones who are going to be running this company from now on."

The applause swelled again as Tom raised his hand to dismiss the meeting, then left the podium.

As the crowd dispersed, the blonde woman came up to Tom. "I'm Isobel," she said. "I work in accounting."

"Isobel," Tom said. "Nice to meet you."

"You know, there's another thing about the advice process you didn't mention," she said.

"Yeah?" Tom asked.

"Well, you talk about how it's more fun when you get to make the decisions. And that's true," she said. "But it's fun to give advice, too. You should ask my mother-in-law. She can't stop giving it."

Tom laughed. Isobel smiled.

"So, using the advice process, the decision-maker makes better decisions." she said. "But it's also a way for the rest of us to have some of the fun of making them, too."

"You're right," Tom said.

"I don't know if I'll even care whether they take my advice," she said. "It'll be nice just to know someone took the time to listen. It's like with my son. Maybe I want him to be an accountant, but he thinks about it, and he knows he wants to be an architect. I tell him it's hard work, the school's expensive, the hours are bad. If he still chooses to do it, at least I know he didn't go into it blind. That was a choice he made. It might not be what I would choose, but I still feel good. He thought about it, and he heard me out."

Tom nodded. "I hope you're right," he said.

"I can't wait," Isobel told him. She moved off into the crowd.

Tom went over to Jim. "What do you think?" he said.

Jim didn't exactly give him a round of applause. "If it heads off a problem like the one we've got with our useless polymer, I'm all for it," Jim said.

"The decision-maker process was already working before this problem with the polymer," Tom told him. "With this advice process in place, we'll have all kinds of eyes on every decision. I can't see what could go wrong."

"That's exactly what I'm afraid of," said Jim.

14.

A Giant Leap

"I never really understood it," said the researcher, a young, dark-haired woman. She sat at one end of a conference room table, along with about a dozen members of the research and tech teams. Mike had invited Tom and Jim to the research wing to hear a handful of reports on the effects of the decision-maker process on his area over the past several months.

"I wasn't trained in how our computer models translated into real-world prototypes," the researcher said. "I'd never done it. It didn't make sense for me to try to direct that part of the process. And now that we've given those decisions to Sharon, our turnaround time on the models has been cut by a third."

"I'm impressed," Jim said.

Already, team members had reported bumps in efficiency and drops in cost. But perhaps most important was the

change Tom saw in the way the researchers and techs inter-
acted during the meeting. When he'd first come to the company, they hadn't been exactly hostile, but there had been
a clear divide. Techs tended to cluster with techs, and researchers tended to cluster with researchers, even when they
gathered as a group. Today, though, they were mixed together at the table. Techs often leaned over to talk to researchers,
and researchers frequently glanced at techs for confirmation.

"That's great," Tom said, smiling at Sharon.

"I'd love to pretend I'm some kind of genius," Sharon said.
"But it was really common sense. I just never had permission to make the decisions before."

"Still," Tom said. "Excellent work."

"I'm just glad it's going better than your last visit to the
lab," Mike said, with a slightly rueful smile.

"This is great," Tom said. "You've accomplished a lot here."

"We're not quite through yet," Mike said. "Jogen?"

A young researcher with a mop of brown hair and a pair
of Buddy Holly glasses started, then shuffled the papers in
front of him. "Well, I'm relatively new here," he said. "And
so is Ken." The lab tech next to him, a young Asian man,
nodded his greeting. "They put us both on testing for the
MedTec Proto line. I guess they figured we couldn't get into
too much trouble there, since it was already designed."

Laughter rippled through the room.

"I have to say, I wasn't crazy about working with a tech at
first," Jogen said. "I wasn't sure what a tech could bring to
the process. Researchers, I guess we tend to think that techs
are—"

"Stupid?" Ken said, when Jogen hesitated.

Jogen nodded, with a grin that showed he was taking ribbing from a friend.

"That's okay," Ken said. "Techs all think researchers are lazy. Jogen's not, by the way."

"How did the decision-making process teach you that?" Tom asked, curious. He hadn't been trying to build camaraderie among his people when he came up with the idea. He'd just been trying to give individual people more satisfaction in their own jobs.

"I guess—" Jogen said, and stopped to think. "It started when Ken got to make some of the decisions. I used to just go down there and tell the techs whatever I wanted them to do. It wasn't much of a conversation."

"No," Ken said, with some feeling.

"But with the process," Jogen went on, "Ken had his own decisions to make. I had to talk to him in order to make my own decisions. And he'd come to me sometimes for advice, with questions. They were good questions. And good decisions. I realized, this guy isn't stupid."

"And when I realized how much Jogen actually knows about design and materials, and got a look at everything he has to do on the research end, I realized he's not lazy," Ken added.

"Interesting," Tom said. "That's an outcome I never expected."

"That's not our only outcome," Jogen said.

"Oh?" Tom asked.

Jogen pressed a button on his computer. A set of line drawings appeared on the screen on the far wall of the room.

"What are we looking at here?" Jim asked.

"Well, I've always liked to play around with things a bit when I'm doing the modeling," Ken said. "I mean, I follow instructions. I always turn in what they ask me to. But it's not much fun, just following other people's directions all the time. So every now and then, I'll just play with something—turn it upside down, or make one part twice as big—before I turn it in. I just never used to show what I did to anyone."

"Until I came down one day while he was in the middle of modeling one," Jogen said.

"I wasn't wasting company time," Ken said quickly, glancing at Jim. "I had a build I was watching. I was killing time until it was finished."

"I asked him what it was," Jogen said. "Since it didn't look anything like any of the devices I knew he was working on. And when he handed it to me, I suddenly realized he'd solved a problem I'd been working on since I got out of graduate school."

"I wasn't trying to solve it," Ken said. "I was just playing around."

"Jogen's not the only one who's been trying to solve it," Mike broke in. "The whole industry has. You want to tell them how it works, Jogen?"

Jogen nodded, and went on to explain. Ken hadn't realized it when he'd modified the MedTec design, but Jogen had recognized that the new device would be an ingenious improvement on one of the industry's most popular standard surgical aids.

"But we don't make surgical aids," Jim said.

"I know," Jogen said. "That wasn't the purpose of the original design. Ken was just experimenting. But I could see what he'd done, because I worked on surgical aids in graduate school."

"And this isn't just a step forward for the technology," Mike interjected. "It's a giant leap. If we introduced a product like this, I don't know that our competition would still be in business at the end of the next decade."

"Surgical aids are big business," Jim allowed.

"We brought this to you as soon as we worked up the drawings," Mike said. "So I haven't done much in the way of market analysis. But I was able to find sales figures for competitive devices over the past year."

A column of numbers appeared on the screen in place of the drawings. The total at the bottom was almost as large as MedTec's gross receipts for the previous year, across all categories.

"You've got my attention," Tom said.

"But we don't make surgical aids," Jim repeated, more insistently.

"It'd be a big decision," Mike said. "And we know we don't have the authority. So we thought we'd ask you: who is the decision-maker on this?"

"Well, it affects the whole company," Jim began. "I think it's obvious that Tom and I, as executives—"

"Sure," Tom broke in. "But who's closest to the decision? The research team already knows more about this device than either of us. They're the ones who came up with the idea in the first place. It seems obvious to me that we ought to put this in the hands of someone on the research side."

Jim's jaw tightened. "You know what?" he said. "I think we ought to let all of these people get back to work. It's been a good meeting," he said, glancing around the table. "Great work, all of you. We'll be in touch. Thank you. "

Startled, the researchers and techs began to collect their things and rise to go.

Tom turned to Jim. "I really think—" he began.

Jim stood up and jerked his head toward the door. "We need to talk," he said. "Now."

15.

A Decision This Big

But on the walk back from research to the executive offices, Jim was dangerously silent.

He didn't say a word as Tom followed him into his office, where he circled behind his desk and sat down. "Shut the door," he said.

Tom pulled the door closed behind him and went over to Jim's desk. Neither one of them sat down.

Jim crossed his arms. "I'm not sure how to say this," he said.

"Just say what's on your mind," Tom said. "We're partners. I can take it."

Jim sighed. "Look," he said. "We always said that as partners, we need each other. Right?"

Tom nodded warily.

"You're the one with the bright ideas," Jim told him. "The vision guy. That's great. Can't run a business without it. But the vision guy needs to work with someone who has a more cautious leadership style. That's me. It's my job to make sure we don't go off the rails with these new ideas."

"Well, I wouldn't say—" Tom began.

Jim raised his hand. His expression made it clear he wasn't in the mood for interruptions.

"You've always told me that you want to know what I see that you don't see. You've always told me to raise the alarm if I see red flags down the road. Well, I see red flags. I'm raising the alarm. You're talking about letting an entry-level researcher decide strategy for the entire company. Our company. The company we both have our life savings in. Not to mention Helen Harris's investment.

"I want our people to be happy just as much as you do," he went on. "And I'm not blind. I see the usefulness of some of these ideas. But, bottom line: this is our investment, not some researcher's. It's our money on the line, and Helen's. I've sold Helen a lot of your ideas. Ones I'm not even sure of myself. But I'm not on board with this one.

"You've been talking a lot about who should make a decision. Who's closest to it. Who it's going to affect. Well, we're the ones who have the most at stake here. It's our money and our names on the line. We're the ones who should decide."

"I hear you," Tom began, treading carefully. "But if it weren't for these new ideas, we wouldn't even have this opportunity to begin with. It's the decision-maker process that sparked this development in the first place. And it's an amazing opportunity. Even if it's half as good as they think. Even if it's a quarter. You've got to see that."

"I told you I see the benefits," Jim said. "But I still don't think it's appropriate to have someone outside leadership make a decision of this magnitude. And I *know* Helen won't."

"Do you really think you and I will make a qualitatively better decision than Jogen would?" Tom asked.

That stopped Jim for a moment.

"He's been at the company longer than we have," Tom pointed out.

"That doesn't mean he has the expertise to lead," Jim insisted.

"Neither do we," Tom said. "If we make this decision, what's the first thing we'd do? Start talking to area leaders. Gathering opinions from the different sides. Weighing them against each other. It's the advice process. All I'm suggesting is that he do it, not us. Do you really think that, confronted with all the same facts we'd gather, he'll make a different decision?"

"I don't know," Jim said.

"I doubt it," Tom said. "And we're some of the people he'll have to ask. It's not as though we won't have a say in the process. It's just that the decision we make is to let our people make the decision. We can't stop being the leaders. Not even if we want to. As you said, it's our name on the line. But we lead by letting our people make decisions, not making them ourselves."

"Okay," Jim said—not agreeing with Tom, but working through the idea with him now. "You're right. If you and I were making this decision, we'd get a lot of advice. Especially since we're still getting to know the company. And I'm willing to give you the fact that a lot of people here probably know better than you and I do how to run their areas or do their jobs.

"So tell me, why don't we ask all of them? Why give all this responsibility to one single person? Why not put it to a vote? Why not let *everyone* make the decision?"

Tom shook his head. "You can see the benefits of getting advice," he said. "But that's only one part of the process. Casting a vote doesn't give nearly as much satisfaction as making a decision.

"Also, there's no accountability in voting. People don't work as hard to make the right decision, because there's no way anyone can hold them responsible. And people don't feel the same kind of buy-in with a vote that they do with a decision. Even if someone only gets to give advice, they know someone heard what they had to say. They made their case. They had a conversation. They didn't just cast a ballot. People are motivated when they feel they have ownership of what's happening. They don't have that with a vote. If they did, you'd see a lot higher turnout in elections.

"And we're not the only people at this company who have something important at stake," Tom went on. "For us, it's a big financial investment—because we happen to be in a position to invest financially. But everyone else in the company is invested, too. Their jobs and their livelihoods are on the line when a decision like this gets made. And in some cases, those jobs might matter even more to them than our investment does to us. Why shouldn't they get some say in a decision at this level? And who's to say they'd make one that's any worse than ours? Or even any different?"

Jim sighed. He finally sank down into the seat behind his desk. "You're talking about giving this decision to Jogen because he's close to it," he said. "But that's not the only criteria. We need someone with a history of good decisions. And I don't know anything about that guy's history of decision-making."

Tom nodded. "Neither do I," he said, sitting down across from Jim. "That's why we shouldn't make the decision about who makes this one. We should let Mike. He's head of research. He knows his people better than we do."

Jim shook his head. "Wow," he said. "You don't even want us to make *that* call."

"Well," Tom said. "Who would you pick?"

Jim leaned back in his chair and looked at the ceiling. "I don't like it," he said. "But I can't argue with you. You're right. Mike probably knows best."

"We'll talk with him before he does anything," Tom said. "And we won't be the only people he talks to before he chooses. He'll have to get advice, too."

"All right," Jim said. "I'm willing to let this play out. We'll give the decision to Mike. We'll have him use the advice process. Whoever he chooses, we'll let them work out whatever they need to in order to make a decision. But I'm not saying I'll be bound by it. If they come back with something crazy, I'm pulling the plug."

"That's fair," Tom said.

"I'm surprised you gave me that point so easily," Jim said.

Tom smiled. "Well, it's not how I'd like to see it work in the future," he said. "But this is the first time we're going to trust one of our people with a decision this big. And I'm sure they're not going to come in with anything crazy."

Jim shook his head. "Okay," he said. "You've got me on board for one more round. But I don't know what we're going to tell Helen."

"We'll let the process play out," Tom said. "We'll hear what the decision is, from whoever Mike chooses. And then we'll tell Helen it was our decision."

Jim raised his eyebrows.

"Because it is," Tom said. "We won't have made it the way another executive might have. But that doesn't mean it wasn't our decision."

"You really think that's honest?" Jim asked.

"I think it'd be dishonest to pretend it wasn't our decision," Tom said. "Like you said, we're the bosses. We're the ones ultimately responsible if something goes wrong—not whoever we chose to give a decision to. We can't ever really give up that responsibility, not even if we wanted to. Our new process brings more minds to the problem, and it gives more satisfaction to our people. But these are still our decisions. We choose to give them to our people. And that's how we make our decision."

"Well, it'll be interesting to see what they come back with on this," Jim said.

"They'll do just as well as we could," Tom said. "If not better."

"We'll see about that," Jim said.

16.

See How It Works

"Hey, buddy!" Tom's friend Sam bounded up from the restaurant booth where he'd been waiting to meet Tom. He was a big guy, blonde, tan, with whitened teeth and an athlete's build. The back thumping he gave Tom in greeting was so vigorous that it took Tom a minute to catch his breath as the two of them sat down in the booth.

"So what has it been?" Sam asked. "Has it been a year?"

"At least," Tom said. "Maybe longer. We were tied up with the acquisition for months. I was hoping things would slow down after that, but then you close and suddenly you've got a new business on your hands."

"I know the feeling," Sam said. He'd worked with Tom and Jim at the company they had left. In fact, he'd struck out on his own a few years before Tom and Jim had. Sam's success in starting his own company was one of factors that spurred Tom and Jim to strike out themselves.

Tom nodded. "I'm sure you do," he said.

Sam flipped open the menu. "So," he said. "Argentinian food? I was used to our burger lunches. Or fish and chips."

Tom laughed. "It's a long story," he said. "I'm not choosing the restaurants for my lunch meetings anymore."

Sam closed the menu. "Well," he said. "It doesn't take long to choose your order here. Just steak, steak, or steak. So I've got time."

Tom glanced down the list of lunch options, realized Sam was right, made a quick selection, and set his menu aside.

"I've got my admin choosing restaurants for me," he said. "That's the short explanation."

"What's the long one?" Sam asked.

"Well," Tom said. "We've been playing with some new ideas about how to do business."

"Love it," Sam said. "I can't get enough of this stuff. I read business books like my wife reads romances. So what are your new ideas?"

Tom paused for a minute, trying to figure out how to sum up all the ideas, trials, and failures of the past months in a few words. "They're about people," he said.

Sam looked at him like he was still willing to listen, but there better be a whole lot more where that came from.

"The way people get treated at work," Tom said. "At most jobs. There's a set of assumptions behind it. Most businesses assume people are only motivated by fear and money. They treat their people like kids, or machines. They assume people aren't creative. They assume they should all be rewarded and punished exactly the same way. And they assume they can't be trusted."

"Yep," Sam said. "I see all that."

"That wasn't true about us," Tom said. "You, or me, or Jim. It's why we went out on our own."

"Right," said Sam. "But it's true about some people."

Tom raised his eyebrows to show he didn't agree. "Well," he said, "when I got to MedTec, I started thinking about it. And I realized, I don't believe it's true about everyone else, either. So now we're working with a different set of assumptions. We assume our people are creative. We assume they're unique. We assume they want to be part of something that matters, and that they have a desire to contribute. We believe they're capable of learning. And we believe they can be trusted with decisions."

"What kind of decisions?" Sam asked.

"All of them," Tom said. "Think about it. We pretend top people should make all the decisions. But up at the top, we're the furthest from what's really going on. The people who really do the work, they're the experts—at doing their own jobs. So we're giving them the power to make decisions."

"Then what's left for you to do?" Sam asked.

"We decide who makes the decisions," Tom said. "That's our job as leaders—the same way coaches decide who plays, but they don't play the positions themselves."

Sam leaned back in the booth, interested but skeptical. "So how has that been going for you?" he asked.

"It's had its ups and downs," Tom said. "I guess it's your call whether you like Argentinean better than burgers. But my admin is starting to enjoy her job for maybe the first time in her life. We saw a jump in sales when we gave individual salespeople the power to make decisions on deals without clearing them with the main office first. And research just came up with a pretty amazing concept for a new product. We're still deciding if we want to go in that direction, but pushing decision-making deeper into the company is what sparked it. It forged connections between people in different areas, which led to a research breakthrough."

"You're not seeing any problems?" Sam asked. "I mean, I like the idea, but I'm not sure I'd trust some of my people to just start making big decisions on their own."

"Yeah, we did have some problems," Tom said. "And they came from people making decisions on their own. So we've added an advice process."

"I haven't heard of that," Sam said.

"It's pretty simple," Tom said. "The manager of a team chooses someone to make a decision. It's that person's decision, and they're responsible for the consequences. But before they make the decision, they need to get advice. Someone above them, someone below them. People who have faced a similar problem or worked on a similar project. The bigger the decision, the more advice they get. In the end, I think they're probably making better decisions than a CEO might.

"We're still rolling out the advice process," Tom went on. "But I already see a lot of advantages. The first one's obvious: a lot more eyes on any given decision, which is never a bad thing. I call it "best knowledge"—with the advice process, the decision is based on the best knowledge available, rather than one person's call.

"And that's not the only thing it does," he continued. "We've found it also pulls our teams together. It improves communication on all fronts. It's not just about getting the right answer. It's about releasing all the power that comes when teams really bond. So asking for advice isn't just a way of getting a better answer. It's a way of getting a whole team involved. People get asked for advice, they start to feel ownership. And that means everyone who offers advice starts working for the success of the project, just as if it were their own."

Sam nodded, clearly intrigued.

"Some of it's less obvious," Tom told him. "But I think there will be some significant long-term gains, too. When you watch someone go through the advice process, they become the expert on whatever they're researching. All that new information flows into every other decision they make. It means our staff is constantly learning. And it frees the company from being dependent on the leadership to make every decision. Used to be, if Jim or I were out for some reason, everyone was stuck, waiting for our decision. Now we're more nimble. And it gives us a deep bench."

"And you saw a sales spike?" Sam said. "When you rolled all this out?"

"Yes," Tom said. "But that's not really what we're focused on. We want MedTec to be a healthy company. It's got to be, to stay in business. But this isn't about the bottom line. It's about our people."

"They're great ideas," Sam said, with his typical enthusiasm. "Really great. I bet you're seeing efficiencies, too. If you put people in charge of their own areas. Less waste, right?"

"Some of that," Tom agreed.

"How's that flowing into your financials?" Sam asked.

"Expenses have dropped slightly," Tom said, slightly uncomfortable with Sam's focus on the numbers. "This quarter."

"Love it," Sam said. "You're better than the last airport business book I read. Listen," he said, leaning in. "How do you feel about somebody else trying out some of these ideas? I'd love to take what you're doing and see how it works at my company."

Tom's mouth snapped shut in surprise. It had never occurred to him that his ideas would go any further than MedTec. But he felt a wave of gratification at the idea. The only other people he'd talked with much about the ideas were Jim and Sophia, and both of them gave him plenty of pushback. It felt great that Sam thought the ideas were good enough to take back to his own company.

"Well, sure," Tom said after a minute. "Sure, anything you think might be useful. You're welcome to it. They're not trade secrets. They're just some things we're trying out."

"It sounds to me like you've got some very strong business outcomes," Sam said. "Don't sell yourself short."

Tom felt another pleasant glow of pride. It was hard to tell if you were making headway in the midst of change, he thought. With all the conflict with Jim, all the setbacks and hard work, maybe this was just what he'd needed: a buddy with the perspective to remind him that, from the outside looking in, he was actually making good progress.

"Thanks," he said.

"Thank you," Sam said. "I think you just made a considerable contribution to my bottom line."

The waitress appeared at the table. "Are you gentlemen ready to order?" she asked.

"Absolutely," Sam told her. "I'll have the steak."

17.

Human Resources?

"I've thought a lot since we last talked," Angela said, settling into one of the chairs across from Tom's desk, beside Jim. "I've looked at what we're doing in human resources. I've gotten advice from team leaders and team members. And then I thought some more."

"That sounds good," Tom said.

"So what have you been thinking?" Jim asked.

Angela took a deep breath. "I think we should dismantle the human resources department," she said.

Jim's eyebrows shot up. He gave Tom a look of disbelief.

Tom nodded, trying to keep his voice even. "Tell me more," he said.

"First of all," Angela said, "the more I think about it, the less I like the term 'human resources.' It makes it sound like people are just another resource, like metal or energy. It's a holdover from the bad old days. This idea that people are like interchangeable parts, or that they're even any kind of parts at all. Instead of people."

"Fair enough," Jim said. "But we can fix that by coming up with another name. Why do you think we should dismantle the whole department?"

"I've been watching some of the things that have been happening in the company since we introduced these decision-maker ideas," Angela said. "It's impressive. When we release decisions to people, I'm seeing more personal investment, higher satisfaction, better communication—and a lot of times, better decisions. I believe in it. But right now, human resources still holds a lot of important decisions. Ones that we're probably not the most qualified to make. Why should we hire and fire, when we're not the people who have to work with the new team members? Why should we do strategic planning for the whole company, when we know less about what's happening in any given area than the team members in them? Why should decisions about vacation and leave be made centrally, instead of within the teams they affect?"

"All good questions," Tom said.

"I want to release as many HR decisions as possible to the teams themselves," she said. "And I want to get rid of the company handbook. We'll keep something up to date for legal purposes, but we're not going to use it to guide decision-making. The company handbook is specifically designed to keep people from asking questions. That's why you put the answers all down in one place. But once you do, nobody asks questions anymore, even the ones you want them to: 'Why do we do this?' 'How we could do it better?' They teach us to set up a company like a machine you start up and then walk away from. But people aren't parts in a machine. I want them coming up with the right answer for them, that day, not the answer someone else came up with five years ago."

"Okay," Jim said. "But we don't want people to have to re-invent the wheel every time."

"Of course not," Angela said. "That's what the advice process is for. But in the advice process, you learn from other people, not from a static document. The other person can make sure you really understand what they're telling you. And if they're not making sense, you can tell them that. Unlike an employee handbook. Which is not to say I've never seen someone muttering at their employee handbook."

"All right," Tom said. "I'm sold. No more employee handbook. But tell me: when we talked before, you wanted to know where you'd fit in if we dismantled the human resources department. Now you're the one advocating we do that. If we dismantle HR, where do you see yourself in the company?"

"I've given quite a bit of thought to that," Angela said. "You'll still need me. I'm an expert on insurance and compliance. When we start to roll these new policies out, we'll be walking into a regulatory minefield. I'll still be useful in an advisory capacity. And that's not all I plan to do."

"No?" Jim said, with a somewhat sardonic look at Tom.

"No," Angela repeated. "We'll still need people to support the teams as they take on their new responsibilities. And once they're up and running, we'll still need people to make sure the advice process is understood, and to provide accountability to make sure it's being used to the fullest. I'm thinking of something like an advice advocate. Or an education department."

"I like it," Tom said. "But it sounds like a delicate balance to me. You don't want to get in the way of the relationship between a team member and a leader. Good communication between them can drive our business—or sink it. We want accountability. But we don't want to interfere."

"Right," Angela said, and laid a sheaf of papers on his desk. As Tom picked it up and began to leaf through it, she went on. "This is a mock-up of a survey I've designed to make sure MedTec stays on track with both decision-maker ideals and business outcomes," she explained. "It doesn't insert us directly between the team member and leader. But it gives everyone in the company a chance to weigh in on a regular basis about how well things are working in their areas. We hear from everyone, but we don't get in the way of them communicating with each other. This draft of the survey asks questions about how well we're living up to the commitments we've made about decision-making in the company. But it also tracks manufacturing and lab operations, company assets, and sales backlog."

"It helps us gauge the health of the company," Tom mused.

Angela nodded. "I'd like to institute comprehensive surveying at MedTec, using something along these lines," she said. "It'll be a kind of large-scale version of the advice process. And it will also tell us if the advice process is working in other areas—both whether people are responding to it on a personal level, and what outcomes it's having on the business end."

"Angela," Tom said, and laid the survey down on his desk. "You're hired."

Angela grinned.

"You've done an incredible job with this," Tom said. "I'm not sure I could have done this myself. When I came up with these ideas, I knew I wasn't in any danger of losing my job. I own the place. It's pretty hard to get rid of me. But you've done something even more impressive. You've embraced these ideas despite the risk to your job. And you haven't just created a new strategy for the company. You've made a new place for yourself."

"I think it's going to be even better," Angela said. "I got into this field because I like working with people. But it hasn't really been about working with people. It's been about working with policies and procedures. Now I'll get to do what I wanted to in the first place: connect with people. Help them connect with each other. Connect them with work they really love to do, and make sure they have the tools to do it."

"Wonderful," Tom said. He leaned back in his chair, with a feeling of satisfaction over a meeting gone well.

Beside Angela, Jim shook his head, looking relieved.

"One other thing," Angela said.

"What's that?" Tom asked.

"The budget," Angela said. "It's going to need to be transparent."

Jim lurched forward in his chair. Tom planted his elbows on the desk. Apparently, the meeting was not over.

"Why do you say that?" Jim asked.

"We're talking about giving teams some major decisions," Angela said, turning to him. "Hiring, firing. Strategic planning. Purchasing. What's the primary factor in many of those decisions?"

"The budget," Jim said, but he hardly sounded convinced.

Angela nodded. "We can't send someone into a salary negotiation with a new hire if they don't understand the bigger picture. We can't talk about raises within a team if they don't understand budgetary constraints."

"We can't involve our people in strategic planning if they don't understand how their plans intersect with the overall budget," Tom continued for her.

Jim shot him a look that was half exasperation and half betrayal.

Angela nodded again. "Exactly," she said. "I toyed with the idea of giving people limited access to the budget. Salary ranges in a salary negotiation, for instance. In some cases, it might work. In just about every case, though, I think it'd work better if they had all the information, rather than just a partial view."

Tom shook his head. "I didn't see this coming," he said. "But it makes sense. How can they make good decisions if they don't have some of the most important information?"

"It seems to me that it fits with everything else we've done," Angela agreed.

"You know what?" Jim said. "I don't usually get into these discussions unless they start to affect the numbers. But this conversation is definitely about the numbers." He forced a smile for Angela. "Thanks so much for all this work you've done," he said. "Tom and I are going to need a bit of time to talk it over."

18.

The Plan

The door had barely shut behind Angela when Jim got to his feet. "Look," he said. "I've come this far with your ideas. I'm willing to put out from shore a bit, especially if I can see a clear way to row back to land. But this isn't one of those decisions we can unmake if we don't like the consequences," he told Tom, his jaw set. "If we let out our financial information, we can't ever take it back. The rumors could last for years, even if the actual numbers change."

"Not if we keep giving our people the facts," Tom said.

Jim shook his head. "No one runs a business with complete financial transparency," he said. "And there are reasons for that."

"No one but bosses get to make decisions in other companies," Tom said. "So they're the only ones who need the information. But if we want our people to make good decisions, we have to give them all the data."

"I can see having them work out area budgets," Jim said. "But budgets in other areas? Do we really want to deal with complaints about why this one's bigger than that?"

"If people get a chance to really see what the other side is dealing with," Tom said, "I don't think there will be nearly as much discontent as you get when the financial details are kept in a black box."

"What about salaries?" Jim asked. "It doesn't get much more personal than that."

"Well, for one thing, if they can see the whole budget, they'll be able to see how the decisions they make about efficiency in other areas affect how much we've got left to pay them. And let's be honest. Everyone knows about salaries in a department anyhow. They just don't have the power to change it. With this system, if something's not fair, people won't just sit around and gossip about it. We can work it out."

"They'll get a shock if they see our salaries," Jim said. The two of them had agreed to take bare minimum pay during the first year and plow any profit back into the business. This meant that, despite the fact that they were owners, they were making significantly less than many of the area leaders, and even less than some of their top researchers.

"That could be good," Tom said. "Most people in a company think the bosses are just sitting up in their offices, creating hassles for everyone else and pulling down fat salaries and bonuses."

"And a lot of times they're right," Jim said.

"Sure," Tom said. "But not here. And our people don't know that, because we haven't told them. I don't think revealing that fact is going to hurt us. I think it's going to help. They'll realize they're not the only ones who have skin in the game. And that we're not asking them to weigh the consequences of their financial decisions when we haven't made sacrifices for the business ourselves."

"You really want to do this, don't you?" Jim said.

"It's not a matter of what I want to do," Tom said. "It's a matter of what makes sense."

"Well, I'm still the CFO," Jim said. "Where does my opinion figure in all of this?"

"Your opinion on this is the most important one in the business to me," Tom said. "Which is why I think you should choose the decision-maker on it."

Before Jim could answer, Tom's phone rang. He glanced down at it. It was Vanessa's line. "This will be Jogen," he said, and picked up the receiver.

"I have Mr. Vasantkumar here for you," Vanessa told him.

"Thanks," Tom said. "Send him on in."

Tom and Jim both rose as the researcher came through the door. Jogen shook both their hands with a mixture of exhilaration and nervousness. The three of them settled into their chairs, Tom behind his desk, Jogen and Jim on the other side.

"Well," Tom said. "Congratulations on being decision-maker on the strategy surrounding our possible new product launch. We could see you had the expertise from your background, but Mike says he also believes in your ability as a decision-maker. We're looking forward to hearing what you've come up with."

Jogen smiled. "Thanks," he said. "Actually, I asked for this meeting to get your advice. But first I'd like to tell you some about what I've already done."

"That sounds like a good start," Jim said.

Jogen took a deep breath. "Well, when I became decision-maker on this project, I started to really think about the advice process," he said. "You're supposed to ask the people who have expertise that might affect the decision, and people who will be affected by what happens. When I got to thinking about it, I realized that this decision will affect everyone in the company. So I decided to talk to everyone in the company," he concluded.

"Wow," Jim said, his friendliness slightly strained. "That sounds like it would take up a lot of time."

"It does," Jogen said. "But it's been worth it. Some people didn't have a lot to add. Some people did. But they were all glad I asked. And I've been getting all kinds of input I didn't even know to ask for. Some of the best ideas came from people you would never expect. That's kind of where this whole new product idea came from, in the first place—just a tech playing around with something no one asked him to play with."

"How does spending all this time affect the rest of your work?" Jim asked. "As a researcher?"

Jogen gave him a slightly nervous glance. "It's taken some time away from it," he said. "But Mike understood that when he made me decision maker. And I'm still involved in all of my projects."

"Even by conservative projections, this could be a huge

win for us," Tom told Jim. "It's hardly a bad investment to get this kind of feedback and buy-in from our people."

"They haven't all been individual meetings," Jogen added. "In fact, I don't think those always work the best. Some people want to sit down and have a conversation with you. But some people do better in groups. I figured this out along the way. I'd just finished talking to one woman in manufacturing. She'd told me she didn't really have any bright ideas. But then when I started talking to another guy nearby, she heard what he was saying and disagreed. The two of them wound up arguing for ten minutes, and they finally came up with an idea neither of them would have started with on their own. After that, I started setting up these kind of focus groups. To see what happens when people put their heads together."

"Interesting," Tom said. "So what have you got?"

Jogen handed each of them a thick report. "You can see the outline of the plan in the first few pages, with all the supporting data beyond. It's interesting. I thought the big challenge was going to be manufacturing, but it turns out it's actually going to be the market. Our machines are already configured to make similar devices. That's why Ken had the pieces to tinker with in the first place. The real trick in manufacturing will be sourcing some new materials, because the device's tolerances will be different if it's put to different use than the original design intended."

"Sure," Tom said.

"As you can see, that'll be our primary financial risk. Some of the materials will be significantly more expensive. We can drive that price down by ordering larger quantities.

I thought originally that we could estimate materials needs based on pre-orders, but when I talked with sales, they don't think they can take this to market without samples. Not pro-totypes, but actual samples. Working ones. Preferably free."

"That's pretty standard," Jim said, nodding.

"So we're going to need to make a significant investment in high-cost materials before we can really determine the true size of our market," Jogen concluded. "That said, there is some good news. MedTec doesn't typically make this kind of device. But our current customers already buy them. We don't need to strike out into a new market to find custom-ers. We can begin with our current clients and build from there. I've also fleshed out those rough numbers you saw at our first meeting. As you know, there wouldn't really be any-thing out there on the market that could compete with us. Not initially. But you can see the numbers on comparable products for the past three years. They're substantial. And growing."

Tom glanced down the page to the place Jogen had in-dicated. The projected numbers were even larger than the ones they had seen in the original research team meeting.

"I'm still working on the decision," Jogen said. "But the plan I'm leaning toward is a limited rollout. It's tempting to go big at the beginning, especially because once we intro-duce this we'll have a limited amount of time to capture the market before imitators try to cut into our business. And of course, we'd like to make back the opportunity cost in con-verting to the new product as soon as possible. Conventional wisdom says it will take significant time for manufacturing to ramp up if we start with a limited introduction to the market. But when I talked with manufacturing, I found out some interesting things." He flipped through the notebook.

"'There's what you tell management you can do,'" he read from a set of notes. "'And then there's what you really can do.' That's what one of them said." He looked up.

Tom suppressed a smile. He knew that principle well himself.

"They believe in this project," Jogen said. "They're on board with it. And with this new bonus system that Angela is working on, they know there's something in it for everyone, not just the execs and leaders, if they do well. If we get the kind of orders we're hoping, manufacturing is confident they can ramp up and fill them in a matter of months."

"Months?" Jim repeated.

Jogen nodded. "Ben told me the sales team should go ahead and take as many orders as they can. He'd fill them."

"I'm usually a pretty conservative guy," Jim said, flipping through his copy of the report, "but what you've projected here is convincing. I might actually have been a little more aggressive."

Jogen shook his head. "I want to be conservative, too," he said. "So I asked accounting to run some projections on what would happen to the business if we allocate our resources this way and the product fails. We'd survive, but it wouldn't be pretty. And it would put a lot of our jobs in danger. I think the product is going to work. I think it'll actually do quite a bit better than we've planned. But I didn't want to put our people at unnecessary risk if I could help it."

Jim's eyes scanned down the page, taking in the details.

"But I've never set strategy for a company before," Jogen said. "And you two gentlemen have. So what kind of advice would you give me? What do you think of the plan?"

Tom and Jim glanced at each other. It was the moment Tom had promised Jim, when Jim could still veto what the decision maker brought them if Jim didn't like what he saw. Tom tilted his head, giving Jim the floor.

Jogen's finger tapped nervously on the cover of the turquoise binder.

"I think," Jim said, and broke out into a wide smile, "we couldn't have done better ourselves."

Jogen broke out into an answering smile. "Thank you," he said. "That's great. But I don't want to celebrate too soon. One thing that's become clear to me during this advice process: until you make a decision and see how it plays out, you never really know whether it's going to work or not."

19.

The Big Picture

Helen Harris swept into the room, her skepticism unmistakable. A few weeks before, convinced by the decision-making process around the new device, Jim had agreed to work with Angela to bring transparency to MedTec's finances. But when he told Helen, she'd demanded an immediate sitdown with Tom and Jim. And at the sight of Angela in the room along with them, her skepticism seemed to deepen into outright distrust.

After they sat down at the conference room table, Tom glanced from Helen to Angela. Angela was smart enough to pick up on Helen's signals, but Angela didn't look worried.

"And how has that gone so far?" Helen asked, with a slightly sardonic air. "Letting the teams set their own budgets?"

"Well," Angela said, handing a sheaf of pages across the table to Helen, "in the short term, it's cut costs."

Helen lost her stern expression. Her face registered surprise. "Really?" she asked, and glanced down at the sheet.

"I'd expected to see some efficiencies," Angela said. "But not this many."

"I would have expected that we would already be seeking efficiency in our budgeting," Helen said, with a meaningful glance at Jim.

Jim shifted in his chair. "Of course," he said. "But the reality is that the budget is created by hundreds of decisions at every level of the company. Until now, only owners and executives got to see the big picture. And benefit from any profit. Nobody else was able to see how their spending affects the rest of the company. And they didn't have much incentive to curb it, because we hadn't had a system of profit sharing or bonuses."

"And you have one now," Helen said, in a tone that suggested she wasn't completely thrilled with the idea.

Angela nodded. "Yes," she said. "We've got individual and team bonuses for high performance, plus a profit-sharing plan for the entire company. Coupled with the transparency, it's been powerful. It's not that we'd negotiated bad deals with our suppliers. But when we gave our people responsibility for their own budgets, we saw them go back and negotiate even better deals. When we set the budgets for them, everyone tried to spend everything we allotted in every category, so they wouldn't lose it the following year—whether they needed it or not. Now they're using only what they really need. In some categories, spending has dropped drastically. And that's given us the freedom to make some capital improvements that we didn't think we'd have the cash to do—all within the current budget."

Helen pursed her lips thoughtfully. Then her eyebrows drew together. "And I believe setting their own compensation has been part of this?" she said. "So I imagine you've seen an increase there to offset some of these—" she paused, then gave the word a slightly sarcastic emphasis: "—efficiencies?"

Jim nodded evenly. "Each area has handled it differently," he said. "On the manufacturing side, we've seen a slight rise in compensation, but you're right, it has been balanced by efficiencies they've created in other areas."

"Not at the cost to our product, I hope?" Helen said.

Jim shook his head. "No. They actually renegotiated for slightly higher-quality materials, but at a rate that allowed them to all experience a slight bump in pay. But what's most interesting to me is that in several cases, pay has dropped."

Helen's eyebrows shot up. "Dropped?" she repeated.

Angela nodded. "We're finding that pay isn't the bottom line for many of our people," she said. "We'd had a strict two-week vacation policy for entry-level positions, but when we dropped it, we discovered that many of our people value some things more than pay. Flexibility. Vacation time. Some people would rather have more time with their family. They want to get home earlier in the day. And when we offer them those things, they're more productive when they're here."

"Tell her about the research team and their new machine," Tom prompted.

Angela smiled. "That's right," she said. "This is one of Tom's favorite stories. We've got a research team that's been agitating for a new machine since before the company was sold. When we gave them control of their budget, they actually froze their own salaries until the next fiscal year so they could purchase it."

Tom grinned. "They're like kids with a new toy," he said. "You should see them. And it's opened the door to a whole new field of research."

Helen looked down at the columns of numbers in front of her. "And how much are all these—toys—costing the company?" she asked.

"You can see the year-over-year numbers there," Jim said. "It hasn't been very long, but we have several months worth of data to compare."

Helen scanned through the pages, then looked up. "Well," she said, "they look all right."

"They're slightly better than last year's, in fact," Angela pointed out.

"For the moment," Helen allowed. "But we don't know the long-term effects, in terms of making these big purchases, and losses in productivity from all this additional vacation and flex time."

"We haven't seen losses so far," Jim said.

"I'm not sure we know yet what we're seeing," Helen said. "I can tell you one thing. I've been in business for thirty-two years, and I've never seen this degree of upheaval in a company before. You've taken on a lot all at once. New owners. New leadership style. And now a new product. I agree that you've got a handful of nice stories. I'm just not convinced you've got a healthy business."

"Well, I can tell you what we're seeing," Tom broke in. "When we started giving decisions to our people, they started making better ones, and faster ones, everywhere in the company. Costs have dropped. Sales are up. We're seeing fewer accidents, and less waste. And we're seeing higher productivity on the manufacture of our original products, even as we're ramping up the new one.

"But it's with this new product that we're really seeing the decision-maker process come to life. Because we're getting to design it from the ground up. Nearly everyone in the company had a say in taking this new direction, and everyone is energized. Marketing has developed brand-new strategies to take it to a wider audience. Our sales team has been reaching out to so many new clients that sales of our old products have actually increased as well. Our researchers have been probing the viability of several new products after this one. And the techs have reorganized workflow in the lab so that prototyping and testing take significantly less time than they used to.

"The numbers look healthy right now, and they need to stay healthy or we don't have a business at all. But we didn't go into business for the numbers. At least, I didn't. We went into business because we wanted to do something worth doing. And that's what we're seeing."

Helen looked at Jim. "Jim?" she said. "I think it's clear to everyone where Tom stands. I just didn't expect this from you."

Jim took a deep breath. "I hear your reservations," he said. "A lot of them, Tom's heard before—from me. And I've been worried Tom's spending too much time on these ideas, and not enough time on the business." He paused. "But the deeper we get into this, the less I find to argue with. Just like you, I've been watching the numbers. The numbers are good.

"But the thing is," he continued, "now the business is, too. Not just the numbers. I mean the people. They come in, I can see them. They're excited to be here. They feel like they're a part of something that matters, doing something that means something. They're coming up to us with ideas when we walk through an area. They've got schedules and budgets they want us to see, new products they want to show off. A guy just stopped me in manufacturing the other day to show me his productivity numbers. Highest since he'd been working here, he said. And he's been working here for years. Tom's assistant used to worry about scheduling his lunch meetings without his permission. Now she's doing the preliminary analysis for our annual report.

"I know it sounds crazy," he said to Helen. "Because it sounded just as crazy to me. But I'm actually glad you came in today. This is still a good business. You can see it right there in the numbers you've got on the page. But there's something going on here that you can't see from the numbers, no matter how good they are. There's something special about this company. We're doing something that matters here. It's a place people want to be."

Helen shook her head. "This is a business, Jim," she said. "Not an amusement park."

Jim cracked a slight smile. "I know that," he said. "But when people want to be here, it brings out everything they have to offer. Not just *turn that switch* or *turn in that report*. It's powerful stuff. And it's making us a better business."

"Now you sound like me," Tom said, and grinned.

Helen didn't smile, but her face had softened. She looked again at the bottom line of the year-to-year comparisons.

"Well," she said. "As I said, I've never seen this kind of upheaval in a business before. But I've also never seen a business in this kind of upheaval post these kinds of numbers."

Tom's grin got wider.

"I make it a practice to trust my leadership," Helen said. "And I do trust you two. That's why I invested in MedTec. Because of you—not the company or the product. But I'm going to keep an even closer eye on things than I have been." She looked at Jim. "I'd like to see these year-to-year reports on a weekly basis," she said.

Jim nodded. "No problem."

"Thank you," Tom said, standing as Helen rose from the table. "You won't regret it."

Helen shook the hand he offered. But she gave him a warning glance. "Right now, all I'm doing is staying out of it," she said. "I haven't done anything yet."

At the door, she turned and looked back. "And if I have to get involved," she said, "I don't think you'll like it."

20.

A Few Questions

"Tom?" Vanessa's voice crackled over the speakerphone on Tom's desk. "Would you have some time this afternoon to answer a few questions on the report?"

Tom smiled at the receiver. Of all the stories of the decision-maker process at MedTec, this new project of Vanessa's was one of his favorites. For months, she had worked her way through all the well-reviewed and off-the-beaten-path restaurants in town, setting up his lunch meetings. Then she'd started ordering different supplies for the main office. After that, she negotiated a significantly better deal with their phone provider. When the time came to compile data for the company's annual report, Tom requested an appointment with Angela to decide who would be the decision-maker. Vanessa had thought for a moment and then said, "I think I might like to do that."

Tom hadn't hesitated. Vanessa was smart and detail-oriented, and she already saw details on all of the company's moving parts as they flowed across her desk to Tom's. This was exactly the kind of project she could do, and do well. "You're the decision-maker," he'd said. So for the last few weeks, he'd been fielding questions and hashing out ideas on what data to collect and who should analyze it. And he loved the fact that Vanessa, who had never believed she'd have a job she liked, was clearly energized and invested in the process.

Tom pushed the button to speak back. "How about now?" he said.

A moment later, the door to his office swung open.

Tom welcomed Vanessa with a wide grin, but it quickly faded when he saw her worried face.

"Hey," Tom said. "What's going on?"

Vanessa crossed to the chairs opposite his desk and sat down. "I'm working on the section about manufacturing standards for the new product," she said, and stopped.

Tom nodded, trying to keep his composure against a giant wave of impatience to know what exactly was going on. "Yes?" he said. "Is something wrong?"

"It's the advice process," Vanessa said.

Tom felt a rush of relief. When she'd said "manufacturing standards," he'd imagined all kinds of dire outcomes. But the advice-process report was just one of Vanessa's innovations to the standard annual report. To keep track of whether each area of the company was using the advice process, they had created a new section. It blended responses from Angela's surveys with descriptions from team leaders of how the advice process had affected each major

141

step in the development of the company's new products and processes.

"What about it?" Tom asked, his voice relaxing.

"Well," Vanessa said. "As far as I can tell, there wasn't one."

That wasn't great, Tom reflected. But it wasn't a disaster by any stretch of the imagination. "Who was the decision-maker?" he asked.

"Ben Malkmus," Vanessa answered.

Tom nodded again. The fact that Ben might have skirted the advice process in his own domain didn't come as much of a surprise, either.

"I wasn't checking up on him," Vanessa said. "I was just looking for a few details I could write into the report, to show how the process worked. So I went down to manufacturing and talked to a few people to find out who he'd spoken to, and what kinds of things they'd told him."

She shifted in her seat. "Everyone I asked told me he must have talked to someone else," she said. "And when I got done asking everyone, I still hadn't found anyone who really did talk with him."

"Okay," Tom said, and frowned. It might not be a big deal, but he wasn't looking forward to confronting Ben about the problem. His mind began to work. Angela had her share of run-ins making sure the advice process got used. She'd had to get people to ask for more advice, or hold them accountable to the ways they followed it. But they hadn't ever had a manager of Ben's stature totally ignore the advice process.

Vanessa broke in to his thoughts. "I don't want to get anyone in trouble," she said. "But I thought you should know."

Tom forced a smile. "I'm glad you brought this to me," he said.

Vanessa shifted in her chair again. "So what do we do?" she asked.

Tom met her inquiring gaze. "I don't know," he said. "Yet."

21.

Their Own Ideas

Tom found Ben on the manufacturing floor, deep in conversation with one of the line workers. Ben glanced at Tom when he came in, held up his finger, and then finished the conversation while Tom waited. A minute later, Ben clapped the worker on the back and came over to Tom with a big grin.

"Tom," he said. "Good to see you. What brings you down to manufacturing? You looking for a tour of the new tooling we're putting in place? We switched over to the new product in record time. We're running two weeks ahead as we speak. We could actually be putting out the new product by the end of the week, but that would snarl up the delivery schedule. Sales hasn't got anything slated to go out until the end of the month."

"That's great," Tom said. "So tell me, what was it like to use the advice process to roll out the new product? What kind of input did you get?"

Ben's eyes suddenly became wary. He glanced off down the aisle of machinery. "Ah, you know," he said. "Everyone has their own ideas."

Tom nodded. "Like what?" he pressed.

"I keep my ear to the ground," Ben said. "You hear all kinds of things." He gave an unconvincing smile. "You should hear some of them."

"I'd love to," Tom said. "Who did you ask? I know you and I didn't talk, and the advice process calls for talking with someone the next level up. Did you talk with Jim?"

Ben dropped his eyes to the ground. "No," he said. "Nope, I didn't."

"Hm," Tom said, keeping his voice even. "Well, what about around here? Who'd you talk to in manufacturing?"

Up until now, Ben had seemed nervous, but now his expression hardened slightly. He looked at Tom. "Is something wrong?" he asked.

"Not that I know of," Tom said. "I'm just interested in the process. How did it go for you?"

Ben's mouth pressed even tighter, and color began to rise in his face. He glared down the line. Then he met Tom's eyes, this time almost defiant.

"You want the truth?" he asked.

Tom nodded.

Ben folded his arms. "I'm an expert in manufacturing," he said. "I've been working in it all my life. And about half of that time, I was working here. Nobody knows this shop better than I do. And nobody in it knows manufacturing better than me. I didn't need anyone's advice. No offense to you and Jim, but you haven't even been here a year. What were you going to tell me that I don't already know?"

He lifted his chin. "And I'll tell you what," he said. "I made good decisions. We're not just ahead of schedule. We're going to meet design specs for less than anyone expected. And that's what really matters here, right? I've been around long enough to see a lot of management fads come and go. You know, the walk-around style, the seven habits, the grapefruit diet. One thing I notice: what management really wants to see, every time, is a solid contribution to the bottom line. Well, you've got that from me. You don't need to worry."

"So what you're telling me," Tom said, "is that you set the manufacturing standards for the new product without consulting anyone else?"

"Look," Ben said. "I get it. The advice process is a nice idea. Every now and then, it's good to let one of the little guys make a decision. That's fine by me. Might even give morale a little bump, and there's never any harm in that. I can get on board with it.

"But this isn't just any decision," Ben went on. "We're not choosing a new brand of paper towels for the washroom. Manufacturing standards affect everything. It's a big decision, so you gave it to me. And you got that right. Because I know manufacturing better than anyone else in this company.

"I could have gone out and asked some questions, sure. But what would the point of that be? They're not going to tell me anything I don't already know. So I made the calls

I knew were right. And, let me be honest, saved us all a lot of time and energy." Ben suddenly seemed to realize how much he'd just said. A glimmer of uncertainty flickered in his eyes in the silence that followed, but he narrowed his eyes against it and stared right back at Tom.

Tom's blood was boiling, but he managed to keep his voice even when he finally did speak. "The advice process isn't optional in this company," he said. "It's not just about the bottom line. It's not even just about the right decision. It's about the right way to do business."

Ben could barely conceal the curl of his lip at this. "Well, great," he said. "I'll keep that in mind for the future. But as for this decision, it's already been made. Not just made, but implemented. We've been working according to the new specs for weeks. And you may not see it now, but one day you're going to thank me. Trust me on this."

"As I said," Tom repeated, "the advice process isn't optional. On any decision. Including this one. So we're going to run the advice process on this decision, just like any other one."

"But this decision is already made," Ben said, his voice slightly incredulous.

"I understand that," Tom said. "But that doesn't mean it can't be changed. If your decision is as good as you think, the advice process will only bear you out. You're ahead of schedule, right? So it'll give you something to do with all the extra time. We'll work through it together, you and me. And once we've run the advice process, we'll need to talk about the fact that you ignored it."

"And then what?" Ben demanded, his voice rising in alarm.

"And then we'll make any decisions we need to about that, too," Tom said, and walked away.

22.

The New Standards

The woman in the small office at the back of the manufacturing floor looked up when Ben appeared in her door. But her eyes widened when Tom appeared beside him. She had short dark hair, and she was wearing a blue collared shirt and khakis. The sign on her desk read *Nora Stone*.

"Is everything okay?" she asked.

Ben gave Tom a sidelong glance. Then he managed an expression that approximated a smile. "Sure, sure," he said. "We're just here for some—" The smile twisted into a grimace. "Advice."

"On the manufacturing standards for the new product," Tom added.

Nora's eyebrows drew together. "I thought you sent those all down a couple of weeks ago," she said, glancing up at Ben with a worried look. "We already outfitted the line to meet them."

"It's a big step," Tom told her. "We just want to get as many eyes on the decision as possible, before we get too far with it."

"Okay," Nora said, still looking a little confused. "So what would you like me to do?"

Tom looked at Ben.

Ben swallowed. "Do you have any advice?" he asked, with effort. "On the manufacturing standards?"

Nora glanced from Tom to Ben, clearly trying to figure out what the right answer was, given that her boss and her boss's boss were both standing in her office. "You know," she said, "I don't really try to think too hard about the specs when they come down. My job's just to implement them on the line."

Ben glanced at Tom, slightly triumphant.

"Sure," Tom said. "But you have to make decisions about *how* the specs get implemented, don't you?"

Somewhat reluctantly, Nora nodded.

"That's what we're interested in," Tom said. "Any thoughts you have on the best way to implement. You're our expert on that."

"I'm not sure why we'd go back over this now," Nora said, "when we already switched over the line."

"Well, you must be learning things as you do that," Tom said. "About how it's working."

Still reluctant, Nora nodded again.

"That's the kind of thing we'd like to hear," Tom said.

Nora glanced from him to Ben again. "All right," she said after a minute. "But I'll need some time to think about it."

"We're going to talk to a few other people," Tom said. "Why don't you think it over and we'll circle back."

Nora nodded, clearly unhappy. Ben and Tom stepped out of her office, back onto the floor of the plant.

"It's not just my time we're wasting here," Ben told Tom. "It's hers. She's got plenty to do without spending her day going over a set of manufacturing standards that were perfectly good to begin with. And she knows it."

"Who else do you want to ask?" Tom said, ignoring Ben's protest.

"Nora's my right hand. She handles the day-to-day on the switchover, and the government filings," Ben said. "Nobody here is going to know more about the standards than she does."

"What about someone who's actually going to produce the product?" Tom asked. He glanced down a row and caught sight of a familiar figure: Anton Bell, the tech who hadn't been authorized to shut down the machine that had blown when he and Jim had first bought the place. "How about Anton?"

Ben opened his mouth to protest, then closed it again. He shrugged. "Sure," he said. "Let's talk to Anton."

When he saw them coming, Anton looked up with the same blend of surprise and unease that Nora had shown. "Everything okay?" he asked.

"Yeah," Ben said. "Tom here's just got some questions about the new manufacturing standards."

"We're interested in what you think about them," Tom said.

"I told him there wasn't much to think about," Ben said. "We send the specs out, you put them into place on the line."

Anton looked back and forth between Ben and Tom, just like Nora had. Then he folded his arms. "Actually," he said, "it's not quite that simple."

Ben folded his own arms and planted his feet like a prizefighter. "Oh?" he said. "Really?"

Anton didn't flinch. "Yeah," he said. "Don't get me wrong. I'd love it if it were as simple as plugging numbers into a model. That's what they get to do up in research. It's all computer models on high-end software. You want to change something, you just hit a key. The electrons rearrange, and whatever you want comes up on the screen. Down here, it's not so easy."

"What's different down here?" Tom asked.

"We're working with real-life materials," Anton said. "Steel, glass, polymer. You mix it wrong, the temperature changes, the glass supplier starts buying a different kind of sand, and suddenly you've got a real-world product that doesn't live up to your ideal-world specs."

"You're saying we've got factors like that at play here?" Tom asked. "With the new product?"

Anton shook his head. "I'm saying real-world manufacturing isn't as simple as typing a set of specs into a computer model. Take a look at this," he said, turning to his station. He held up a small glass vial, then glanced down at a sheet of numbers. "I'm just running the standard environmental test on this new product."

"That's all taken care of," Ben broke in. "I sent the paper-work to the agency last week."

"Well, I thought I'd run a test myself," Anton said. "The thing is, the test keeps failing." He glanced down at a list of hand-scrawled numbers. "Or we keep failing the test."

"You must be doing something wrong," Ben snapped. "We've never had a problem with environmental compli-ance before."

Footsteps sounded behind them. Anton glanced over their shoulders, and Ben and Tom turned to see who was approaching.

It was Nora, carrying a thick sheaf of papers. "Have you got a minute?" she asked.

"Excuse us," Tom said to Anton. "Thank you."

Anton nodded as Tom and Ben moved down the aisle of machinery to meet Nora.

"What is it?" Ben asked.

Nora shook her head. "It's probably nothing," she said. "It's just, I'm looking over the manufacturing standards, like you asked." She paused.

"Yes?" Ben glowered.

Tom gave her what he hoped was an encouraging nod.

"I've got the results from the compliance testing you gave me to submit to the environmental agency that oversees us," she said. "And I'm comparing them to the specs that came down from research. They're identical."

"Yes?" Ben said again, as if this piece of information only offered further proof that there wasn't any problem to talk about.

"It's just unusual," Nora said. "There's no variation between the research specs and the actual outcomes in manufacturing? Usually there's something. Not much," she added quickly. "But enough that it bears reporting."

"I didn't report any variation, because there shouldn't be any," Ben said, but his bravado was weak.

"Well, great," Nora said. "And is that what we're seeing with our test runs of the product?"

In unison, Tom and Ben glanced back at Anton's workspace.

"We're still bringing a few things up to standard," Ben said.

Nora nodded. "Well," she said. "They'll be testing the prototype we sent them in the next few weeks, to make sure their labs get the same results we did."

For the first time all day, Ben's hard look changed to something like fear. "And if they find some—variation?" he said.

"Well, it's just a matter of how the agency chooses to see it," Nora told him. "As a mistake—or as a lie."

23.

Hear Me Out

"How bad is it?" Jim asked after a long moment.

Standing opposite Jim's desk, Tom shook his head. "I'm not sure we'll know for a while," he said. "It turns out Ben didn't even run the tests. He'd done them for years, and they'd never shown much variation, so eventually he just started filling in the numbers without running the tests. But this time, research called for a new polymer that has a radically different environmental impact. A much more damaging one. Now that we know about it, we can adjust. Fortunately, these were only for the limited rollout of sales samples.

"But you've worked with government agencies before. They can do pretty much whatever they like. If they do anything at all. If we don't come forward about this, I'd say there's a good chance they never discover the problem, and nobody's in any danger of getting hurt."

Jim nodded. "Obviously, we'd never put out a product that would cause that much risk to the environment. Production will conform to the required specs."

"Right," Tom said. "The problem is what the agency will do once they know about the falsified tests. And if we should tell them ourselves, or not."

"They must have some process in place for letting us re-tool if they discover problems," Jim said.

"Yes," Tom agreed. "But we don't know what it is. Have you ever dealt with a project that failed environmental compliance testing before?"

Jim shook his head.

"Me neither," Tom said. "I wouldn't say it's a given that they'll just let us retool and march on. They do reject products. And by the time we come back with something they accept, the damage may be done. This is a brand new product. We need to build trust in the market. Starting with failed marks in compliance testing isn't exactly how I'd like to begin the sales campaign."

"And if we come forward…" Jim began.

"We could nip it in the bud," Tom finished.

"That's if we don't create a huge problem by letting them know there's a problem at all. When we might not need to," Jim observed.

"Yep," Tom said.

"Not to mention the cost of retooling," Jim added. "Any idea how much that's going to run us?"

Tom sank down into the chair across from Jim's desk. "Hard to tell," he said. "I have to say, the failure Anton showed us today didn't look like a minor one. I think we need to go all the way back to research with this. And sales has already started to make commitments for initial shipments."

Jim sighed, leaned forward, and reached for the phone. "I guess we need to start making some calls."

"Wait a minute," Tom said.

Jim paused, his hand on the receiver.

"I'm not sure this is our decision to make," Tom said.

Up until now, Jim had taken in the crisis with his typical even demeanor: the manufacturing snarl, the question of government involvement, the potential financial implications. But now his expression turned dangerous. "What do you mean?" he said, taking his hand off the phone. His voice was eerily neutral, and he clipped out each word almost as if it was its own sentence.

"I'm not sure this is our decision," Tom repeated.

Jim paused for a moment, visibly controlling himself. Then he spoke again. "This decision?" he said. "Whether or not to alert a government agency that we've been massively out of environmental compliance on our new product? Whose decision do you think it is?" he asked.

"I don't know," Tom said. "*That* would be our decision."

"Tom," Jim said. "I've come a long way down this road with you. But this is going too far. I wouldn't be a good partner to you if I didn't tell you that now. This isn't just giving folks a bit more freedom to boost their morale. It's not even giving a researcher the chance make the call on a new product. The decision we're talking about here, it could take the whole company down."

"I understand that," Tom said. "And that's exactly why we shouldn't make the decision ourselves."

Jim leaned in and crossed his arms on the desk. "It wouldn't be responsible to let anyone else make it."

"Hear me out for a minute," Tom said. "We've given our people a lot of decisions over the past months. A lot of really important ones. And it's changed this company, from one that was distressed to one that's on the verge of breaking an incredible new product. That's because we've stopped treating our people like machines and started treating them like people.

"But if we take over this decision ourselves, when we're in trouble, what we'll be telling our people is this: none of those other decisions we let you make really matter, because when it comes down to it—when it really counts—we're always going to take the control back."

"I don't know if you grasp what's at stake here," Jim said.

"I do," Tom said. "It's not just the new product. It's not just a stain on the company's reputation. It could very easily come down to whether we're still in business next year."

"And I'd like to remind you," Jim said, "that no matter who we give this decision to, we can't hide behind that person. When papers get submitted to the government, it's our names on the line. We're the ones they'll come for if anything goes wrong."

"I've got no intention of hiding behind anyone," Tom said. "In fact, this is exactly what I've been talking about. We don't give up responsibility when we give up a decision. We're still the guys in charge. It's just that, instead of standing or falling on what we decide, we choose to stand or fall on what our people decide."

"You really think there's someone in the company who can make a better decision on this than us?" Jim asked.

"You really think there's nobody in the company who could make just as good a decision as we could?" Tom shot back.

Jim shook his head, staring hard at Tom.

Tom stared back at him.

Then Jim sank back in his chair. "I can't believe I'm even considering this," he said. "Who would you pick to make this decision?"

Tom leaned forward. "Anton," he said.

"Who's Anton?" Jim asked.

"The guy who would have kept our machine from blowing the first week we got here, if we'd let him make the decision back then," Tom said.

Jim was quiet for a moment, until he put two and two together. "That guy?" he said, incredulous. "He's a manufacturing tech!"

Tom nodded. "Yes," he said. "And he also identified a problem that none of the managers managed to catch before they sent the initial paperwork on for government approval."

Jim listened, but his look was still skeptical.

"He works directly on the manufacturing of the new product," Tom said. "He's done the testing with his own hands. Repeatedly. So he fits the criteria of being close to the situation. And he'd already started trying to come up with a solution to the problem, before any of us even realized there was one."

Jim shook his head. "This is crazy, Tom," he said. "You really want to give this decision to a manufacturing tech."

"You said yourself we can't give up the responsibility here," Tom said. "I'm not saying we don't give our input. I'm not saying we don't watch the process like hawks. But we've got to give this decision to one of our people, or they're going to know that all the other things we've been saying up to now were only talk."

Jim took a deep breath and let it out. "All right," he said. "I'm willing to give it a try. One more time. We'll let him run the advice process and see what he comes up with. But I'm not signing my name to government documents if I'm not totally comfortable with the solution he brings us."

Tom knew Jim well enough to know how much this had cost him. "Thank you," he said.

"Don't thank me yet," Jim said. "I'm not sure I'm doing either of us a favor. This is the real thing, Tom. I hope you understand that. We're not just experimenting with your new ideas anymore. We're betting the whole company on them."

24.

Every Man For Himself

"It sounds like you've got some real problems over there," Sam said. "And to be honest, I can't say I'm surprised."

Tom took a bite of his cheeseburger. Vanessa had finally run out of palate-expanding options and had sent them to the best burger joint in town. "Well," he said, "Jim and I went over the numbers this morning. Even with all this transition, we're still doing slightly better year over year. We've just got some kinks to work out."

"You sure they're just kinks?" Sam asked

Tom gave Sam a quizzical look. "What do you mean?"

"Well," Sam told him, as he polished off his burger, "you know I liked these ideas of yours when I first heard them. I really did. Enough to take them back and give them a shot at my place. But I've got to be honest. It hasn't gone well."

Tom set down his half-finished burger. "What's been going on?" he asked.

Sam shook his head. "It's been a disaster," he said. "The outcomes you told me about were convincing. And I'm willing to do just about anything to build productivity. So I started letting go of a few decisions, here and there. Giving my people some of the freedom you're talking about. But it's turned into a real free-for-all. Every man for himself."

"What did you try?" Tom asked.

"Well, it's not like I really want to make every decision in the business," Sam said. "Some of them I've always hated. So I started with those. Scheduling's always a hassle, so I passed that down the line. That's one of the things you did, right?"

Tom nodded. "Yeah," he said. "Our people manage their schedules better than we do, and their satisfaction is higher when we let them. It's even caused a slight drop in payroll, because people want more time off than we'd given them, and they're willing to sacrifice a bit of income for more freedom. The crazy thing is, productivity actually grew during the same time. I think when we give them more flexibility about when they're at work, they actually work better when they're here."

"Okay," Sam said, shaking his head. "See, that's what I was hoping for. But it's not what happened at my place."

"What happened at your place?" Tom asked.

"Well, I roll out the idea of flexible schedules," Sam said. "Figure we'll start slow, you know? I explain that I'd like to give everyone a little more freedom, show them a bit more trust. I've heard it drives up productivity. So I put the scheduling in their hands. And immediately one of my managers takes a whole week off. No warning. No prep, that I can see.

Tells everyone in his office they can think for themselves while he's gone.

"And it's a nightmare," Sam went on. "You talk about how your people are making better decisions than you can. Well, I've been working triage on the decisions that got made that week for a month now, and none of them were as good as the ones I could have made myself. People didn't think about the business. They only thought about themselves. They're leaving in the middle of the day. They're missing important calls. They're leaving shifts short-staffed. And it wasn't just the schedule. Some sales rep would take them out to an expensive lunch and suddenly we're buying an inferior product."

"Wow," Tom said.

"Wow is right," Sam told him. "But I wasn't ready to give up. Your story's convincing. And so are the numbers you've told me. And I hate dealing with insurance. Every year, around this time, you start getting the calls, right? Go with us. Better care. Happier employees. Lower rates. And then they send you the documents, and it's like they're written in Greek. They're all advertising different things. It's not like there's any standard scale you can compare them by. Even if you did believe all the promises from the salespeople, which is never a good bet.

"So I think, this is perfect. Another decision I hate making. So I pass it off, just like you said. Give it to one of my managers. Tell her she's free to fly with it. Her decision. She comes back with something that looks pretty convincing to me. Not that I've got any idea, because it's her decision. I sign off on it. We let people know how the coverage will be changing in the next year. And then the complaints start rolling in."

"You always get some complaints," Tom said. "With any change."

"Yeah," Sam said. "But not like this. People are really worked up over it. People who never get worked up about anything. And as I'm listening to them, I can see why. It seems like this insurance plan doesn't work very well for anyone. So I'm looking at the deal, wondering why she chose it. It isn't even saving the company a lot of money. If anything, it's slightly more expensive than what we'd had. I call her in, ask her for the reasoning. And she doesn't even really try to hide it. Turns out, that plan works real well for her and her family. It's got some special provision that picks up payment for a condition no one else covers. Something one of her kids has. She's got some song and dance about how it's just as good as all the competitors, how everyone else should do just fine with it, too. But that's not why she chose it. She chose it because it worked for her family. And it left everyone else swinging in the wind.

"Look," Sam said, leaning over his plate of fries. "I'm not saying I don't understand it. I'm not saying I wouldn't do exactly the same thing in her position. I just can't run a business like that. Luckily, I was able to take us back to our original provider before this new plan kicked in and started a mutiny. But I can't say I'm surprised you're starting to see problems over on your side. Given what I've seen at my place, I'm just surprised you haven't seen more of them."

Tom leaned back in his chair, his appetite gone. "I don't

understand," he said. "We've had some problems at MedTec, sure. But nothing like what you're describing."

Sam raised his eyebrows and gave a sardonic smile. "People are people, no matter where you find them," he said. "Are you sure you're not having the same problems? Maybe you're just not seeing them."

Tom shook his head. "I don't know," he said. He tried to sift mentally through the changes they'd seen at MedTec since they rolled out his ideas: Helen's warnings, Vanessa's worries, the breakthrough on the new product, the positive balance sheets. When he tried to add it all up, he still wasn't sure he had an answer to Sam's question. Especially not with all the trouble Ben's bad call was causing them.

What did the whole situation with Ben prove? he wondered. Was Ben one bad apple in the bunch? Or was he just the tip of the iceberg? Was MedTec secretly full of problems like the ones Sam had run into? Had Tom just been too blind to see them?

Sam spread his hands. "Hey," he said. "It's not a big deal. I'm a guy who's willing to try just about anything to bump my bottom line. And I've tried it all: fancy consultants, one-minute managing, basketball hoops on office doors, blind-folded brainstorming. Your idea seems like a pretty good one in the grand scheme of things—it caused me a lot of trouble, but it didn't cost me any money. I just want to give you fair warning. Sounds to me like you've driven this stuff a lot deeper in your business than I did. So if it went south like this for me, I can only imagine what could happen to you."

25.

That Kind of Boss

Sophia laughed.

That was about the last reaction Tom had expected from her after he laid out the litany of the woes Sam had run into using the decision-maker ideas at his company. Tom and Sophia were sitting side by side on the wooden swing chair in their back yard, where they liked to watch the sun go down and the fireflies come up over the wetlands that lay beyond their property. Tom had been staring out over the twilit grass as he related the story, but now he turned to see her face.

"What's so funny?" he asked, slightly defensive.

Sophia shook her head and planted a kiss on his cheek. "You've got nothing to worry about," she said.

One of the things Tom had always liked about Sophia was the fact that she could handle just about anything, and handle it with a smile. But with their business on the line, and the disaster Sam had just described, her lightheartedness rankled.

"You don't think so?" he said, his voice rising slightly.

Sophia shook her head. "Nope," she said. "What happened to Sam doesn't surprise me at all. I could see that coming a mile away."

"Really?" Tom said, trying to keep his voice even as his irritation increased. He'd been beating his head against the problem ever since he met with Sam that afternoon, and nothing about it seemed clear to him. "But you don't see the same problems coming for MedTec?"

Sophia shook her head again. "No, honey," she said, and squeezed his hand. "You're nothing like Sam."

"I don't see what that has to do with it," Tom countered. "And I'm not sure we're all that different. I'm no smarter than he is. We went into business around the same time. Same industry. That's why we've stayed friends. He's owned his place longer than Jim and I have been at MedTec, but they're pretty similar companies in size and revenue. I don't see why my outcomes should be much different from his."

"Why did you start trying out these new ideas in the first place?" Sophia asked.

Tom stopped for a minute. He wasn't sure what Sophia was getting at. Was she questioning the whole project? If she'd had doubts, why hadn't she shared them before now? He might not always love it when she challenged his ideas, but he'd told her again and again how much he valued her perspective. If she'd seen flaws in his system, why hadn't she told him?

"Why?" he repeated, his frustration evident in his voice.

"Just tell me," she said.

Tom stared out at the fireflies winking over the marsh grass. "Well," he said, feeling a little foolish, "we wanted MedTec to be a good place to work." He paused. "I always hated it when I didn't get to decide anything about the work I did. I guess when I got the chance, I just didn't want to be that kind of boss."

Sophia squeezed his hand again.

"It was never really about money," he admitted. "Maybe we should have paid more attention to that. You don't have a business if you lose control of the financials."

"What about Sam?" Sophia said gently.

"Oh, Sam," Tom said. "He's all about the numbers. Always has been. That's why he caught this stuff so much faster than we did at MedTec."

"No," Sophia said. "That's why he had the problems in the first place."

Tom glanced at her. She grinned. "It's like getting married," she said.

"It is?" Tom said, now thoroughly lost.

Sophia nodded. "Yes," she said. "Think about all the advantages you have because you're married to me."

"There are so many," Tom joked. "It's hard to count."

"You couldn't if you tried," Sophia told him. "But let's just look at a few of the obvious ones. I shop for you. I cook you dinner. I wash your clothes."

"I cook!" Tom protested. "I do laundry."

"Sometimes," Sophia allowed. "But that's not my point.

I come to social gatherings with you. I listen to your problems. I laugh at your jokes."

"That's why I had to marry you," Tom said. "You're the only person in the world who does."

Sophia laughed. "But it's not one-sided," she said. "You do things for me, too."

"I try," Tom said.

"You do," Sophia said. "But that's not why I married you. Think about what would have happened if you'd come to me eighteen years ago and said, 'Look, I need someone to teach me how to do laundry, and I'm tired of having cold SpaghettiOs and Dr. Pepper for dinner. Let's get married. In exchange, I won't complain too much about all the gardening equipment you'll buy over the next several decades, and I'll try to remember to gas up your car from time to time.'"

"That would not have gone well," Tom said.

"No," Sophia agreed. "It wouldn't have. But that's not what you said. You told me you cared about me. I knew you meant it. So I said yes. And you got me—along with all of my many advantages. And that's what happened at MedTec."

"Wait," Tom said. "I'm not married to the business."

"No," Sophia said. "But the people there know you care. That's why you're seeing the improvements you do. People know when they're cared for, and they respond to it. They naturally want to do things for people they know care for them. But they also know when someone's pretending to care for them because they want something. And that's a completely different feeling. It makes you not want to do anything for that person at all. Or it makes you want to get everything you can out of them.

"Sam's that guy," Sophia went on. "He thinks everything is a deal. He just offered his people decisions because he thought it was going to pad his bottom line. But people aren't stupid. They can tell when someone's insincere. Especially someone like Sam. So they treat him just the way he treats them: they look for whatever they can get out of the situation."

"Okay," Tom said. "But at the same time, Sam's right to think about the bottom line. MedTec isn't a family. It's a business."

"That's right," Sophia said. "Which is why it's so strange that so many companies treat their people like children. What's the major thing you and I do as parents?"

"Try to run a tight defense?" Tom guessed.

Sophia gave his leg a playful swat. "No," she said. "We try to teach them to make good decisions. You learn pretty early in the game that, no matter how much you might want to, you can't watch your kids' every move."

"Especially not once there's more than one," Tom said.

"Right," Sophia said. "Very quickly, you realize you can't be there for every decision. So then it becomes about helping them make good ones. You spend your whole life as a parent trying to find the right balance between giving advice, correcting mistakes, letting them go, fixing up the bumps and bruises along the way. All so they can learn to make their own decisions. And then you send them out into the world, and eventually they get a job and go to work—and suddenly, they're treated like children again. They're not supposed to think for themselves. They're supposed to follow rules, to ask permission."

"Huh," Tom said.

"What's sad about it," Sophia went on, "is just how much people have to offer that can never be released by making them follow regulations. How often do the kids come up with an idea neither of us could have dreamed of?"

"About a dozen times a day," Tom said.

"Right," Sophia said. "And all that creativity and energy gets lost when a company tries to dictate a 'company line' on every decision. That's what you're tapping into at MedTec. People are already making their own decisions—a dozen times a day—at work. You recognized that fact. You just brought those decisions into the open, so you understand better what's happening in your own company. The decisions are better because they're not being made in secret. You've strengthened people's natural abilities even more by creating the advice process, so new perspectives get added to the mix. And your people are happier, because you're treating them like adults, not kids."

"This MedTec place you're talking about sounds pretty great," Tom said. "Maybe you should send your kids to work there when they grow up."

Sophia smiled and laid her head on his shoulder. "Maybe I will," she said. "But I'd never send them to work for Sam."

They sat there quietly for a minute, looking out over the wetlands. Then Sophia said, "What about the government reporting on the new product? Have you heard back on that yet?"

Tom shook his head. "I talked with Anton when he came for my advice on it a few days ago, but I haven't heard anything since."

"When will you?" Sophia asked.

"He's coming in with his decision tomorrow."

"And then what?" Sophia asked.

Tom squeezed her hand. "We'll find out."

26.

The Bottom Line

Tom wasn't sure who was more nervous: Anton, him, or Jim.

Jim's face was inscrutable. Tom couldn't tell if he was listening with an open mind, or getting ready to pull the plug and insist on making his own decision after all. And if Tom was honest, some part of him took comfort in the fact that Jim could still take back the decision. If Tom worked his way through the logic, he still believed in letting people make their own decisions. But at this moment, with a problem this big—part of him just wanted things to go back to the way they had always been.

But even more than that, Tom wanted to know Anton's decision. It was all he could do not to lean over the desk and demand that Anton just spit out the answer.

Anton looked up. Tom forced a smile.

"Well, I've talked to a lot of people," Anton said. "And I think there are really two questions we're dealing with. The first one's rewriting the specs so the product meets the environmental standards. That was actually the easy part."

"Really," Jim said, a hint of challenge in his voice.

Anton nodded. "This stuff's been driving me crazy for years," he said. "Research doesn't work with manufacturing on design. They send down specs that would never work in the real world. So manufacturing managers put together a tooling system that will work in real life, but it compromises design. And you know who works it all out in the end?"

Tom raised his eyebrows.

"People like me," Anton said. "I've been patching this stuff back together for years. I had it all worked out, too. How it should go, if anyone would listen. We ought to have a couple people from research work down on the manufacturing floor. Not just paying visits, you know. With their desks there. So other research people have to come pay them a visit and see how things actually work. And then we need a couple people from manufacturing who sit in on the research meetings. Tell them how things work in the real world, not just in their computers.

"So when you asked me to look into all this," he continued, "I didn't just go around and ask manufacturing about all this, and then go up and ask research. I got them all in the same room together. Turns out, the fix is pretty easy. Ben wasn't as up to date as he thought he was on the materials. So we can get a lot closer than we are, even with the current machining."

"Great," Tom said.

Anton nodded. "Research tweaked a couple of other

elements of the design to account for the rest of the changes we need," he went on. "And then I went back to manufacturing and worked through the production line, to see what we were looking at in terms of logistics and retooling. It turns out one of our other techs, Leah, recognized the same issue I did. She built some leeway into the system—just enough to handle the changes we just made between research and manufacturing."

"So what's the impact to the bottom line?" Jim asked, with a hint of impatience.

"Well, if Leah hadn't caught what she did, we'd be looking at building a new machine," Anton said. "As it is, we're not going to be feeling this much at all, financially. The new material's actually cheaper. Changing the design will cost us a couple of cents per part. It'll take us a few weeks to get the right materials in, but we were a few weeks ahead to begin with. All and all, it's a wash."

Tom felt a wave of relief.

"Can I see those numbers?" Jim asked.

Anton handed him a sheaf of columned pages. Jim scanned down them. When he looked up at Tom, his face had relaxed slightly. "These look good," he said.

"That's just our first question," Anton said. "Then we've got the compliance reporting."

Jim laid the stack of numbers down on his knees. Tom leaned forward at his desk. In some ways, knowing the company was in better shape than they'd hoped financially made the question of the government report seem even worse. Before this, they hadn't been sure whether they even had a working company. Now they knew they did—they just didn't know if the government would let them keep it open.

"I talked with a lot of people about this," Anton said. "We're supposed to get advice from people who have made a similar decision before, and I didn't find a whole lot of people who had sent in false reports to the government. But I did find quite a few people who had run-ins with this agency. One woman worked at a company that ran into a similar problem. They hadn't meant to send in false information. It was a glitch in the system. But they didn't catch it for years, and when the agency did, they levied a fine that took the company almost a decade to pay off. Another guy said he worked at a place where the boss was faking the reports. He figured he was so far ahead on the science they'd never figure it out, but they did. And they shut the whole place down. That's how he wound up working for us."

"Any of these stories have happy endings?" Jim asked.

Anton nodded. "A few," he said. "Angela started out in compliance before she moved into HR. She says she's seen them be pretty lenient when a company comes forward with a violation themselves. I talked to everyone I could who had any background in compliance, including a couple of people on our legal team.

"I'd like to say there's a unanimous answer," he said, "but there isn't. Most of the stories I heard, they went pretty easy on people who came forward with a violation. A couple of times, they threw the book at them. Nobody's quite sure why this one and not that one. So, there are no guarantees.

"One scenario," he went on, "would be if our current

paperwork went through and no one ever caught the errors in it. I talked to a guy who worked for the agency a couple years ago, and he said they authenticate the paperwork on a spot-check basis. Not everything really gets re-tested."

"So there's a chance we could slip through scot-free," Tom said.

Anton nodded. "But if they do test the sample we sent—" he said, and paused.

"They throw the book at us," Jim finished.

"And if we do alert them—" Tom began.

"They might throw it at us anyway," Anton said.

The three of them looked at each other for a long moment. Then Tom asked, "What's your decision?"

Anton drew in his breath. He held Tom's gaze steadily. "We tell them," he said. "It's the right thing to do. That's reason enough. And we can't take the chance of them finding out on their own, no matter how small that chance is."

His voice was firm as he said it, but as the silence in the room stretched on after he spoke, his expression turned uncertain.

"At least, that's what I think," Anton said. "But this is a big decision. I'd understand if this is one of the moments where the boss needs to step in and take it over. It might be a relief, actually."

He glanced at Tom. Tom looked at Jim.

Jim shook his head. "No," he said. He clapped Anton on the arm. "This is a tough decision, but it's yours. And you made a good one," he added.

For the first time since he'd sat down, Anton smiled.

Tom sighed and leaned back in his chair, drained.

Anton closed the folder on his lap. "There's just one more question," he said.

Jim gave him a sharp look. "What?" he asked.

"I'm not the decision-maker on this," Anton said, "but a lot of people have asked me about it."

"And what's that?" Tom asked.

"It's pretty obvious to everyone that we were working this advice process after a bad decision had already been made," Anton said. "And that Ben's the one who made it. People are wondering," he said, glancing from Tom to Jim. "What are you going to do about Ben?"

27.

Is That Your Decision?

"Wait," Jim said. "Isn't this supposed to be one of the decisions *we* get to make?"

Angela glanced at Tom. He and Jim had just sat down in her office to get her advice on the situation with Ben.

"Come on," Jim pressed, and turned to Tom, too. "Our people make the decisions, but we choose who makes them. Wasn't that the idea?"

Tom nodded. "Yes, but—"

"I'm afraid it's not quite that simple," Angela said.

"Why not?" Jim demanded.

"Because one of the decisions we made is that decisions about hiring and firing should get made by individuals on teams," she said. "They're in the best position to know who they need, and to identify hires who are a good fit with the team culture. Individuals on teams have held those decisions for the better part of the year. And it's working: turnover, especially for new hires, is way down."

"You're talking about hiring," Jim said. "What about firing?"

Angela took a long breath. "We haven't really faced that yet. We've had some people transition out for personal reasons, and we've had a few teams address some problems with their people. But nothing that resulted in termination."

"Like falsifying government documents?" Jim asked. "Documents that put the whole company in jeopardy?"

"Have we heard anything on that yet?" Angela asked quietly.

"Anton brought it to the agency's attention," Tom told her. "They didn't take any immediate action. It could be months before we know anything."

"In Ben's defense," Angela said, "he believed those numbers were accurate when he sent them in."

"Because he wasn't doing his job," Jim pointed out. "Even if he completely ignored the advice process, he should have done initial tests before sending those claims. Although when it comes right down to it, ignoring the advice process might be a more serious problem."

Tom suppressed a smile.

"What's so funny?" Jim demanded.

"You're starting to sound like me," Tom said.

"My partner," Jim said, "he's a pretty bright guy. *Most* of the time."

"Here's the problem," Angela said. "Teams have been handling their own hiring, firing, and problem-solving. I don't think it's a good decision to take this problem out of their hands. But there's a wrinkle to this one we haven't seen before."

"It's a potential firing," Jim said.

"Yes," Angela said. "But Ben's a leader. So far, when teams have handled hiring and discipline issues, the team leader has led the process or chosen the decision-maker. But in this case, it's the team leader who's at the root of the problem."

"That's exactly what I've been saying," Jim said. "This is one of those very few decisions that Tom and I actually get to make. We lead by choosing the leaders. Ben's a leader. So it's our job to decide whether or not he stays."

"Maybe," Angela said. "But I'm afraid that still might feel to the team like you're taking a very important decision out of their hands. One they know a lot about. And one that affects them more than it affects anyone else."

"Ben's actions have affected everyone in this company," Jim said.

"Yes," Angela said. "But we're talking about what comes next."

Tom shifted in his chair. "Here's an idea," he said. "It leaves the decision in the hands of the team. And it takes into account the fact that Ben's the team leader."

"What's that?" Jim asked.

"Make Ben the decision-maker," Tom said.

Angela and Jim stared at him.

"Have him go through the advice process," Tom went on. "Be the one who gets the feedback from his team on what he did, and what kind of a leader he's been."

"You really think that would work?" Jim asked. "He's still

their boss, after all. And from what I've seen, he hasn't exactly set the bar as the world's greatest listener."

"I think it could work," Tom said. "If we walk through it with him."

A few days later, Ben settled heavily into the chair behind his desk as Tom took the seat across from him. Much of Ben's confidence and bluster were gone, but he looked strangely calm.

Jim had been right: it hadn't been easy to run the advice process about Ben with Ben's own people. But Tom had been right, too: with his prodding, many of Ben's people had opened up. And once they'd started, they'd kept on talking. Over the past few days, Ben and Tom had worked their way across the whole manufacturing floor, asking questions about Ben's leadership: what it was like, how it had affected the people and the company.

The stories they'd heard were sobering. Ben's people had had good ideas, but he hadn't listened to them. They'd tried to improve things on their own, but he'd squashed their attempts—or even punished them. They'd come in to the job excited to be part of a company that made something that mattered. Now they just came into work. Nobody came right out and said that they thought he should step down, but when they described what they'd look for in a boss, their description didn't line up with the portrait of Ben their stories drew.

"I have to tell you," Ben said, pushing back his shock of silver hair. "If I were you, I would have fired me by now."

Tom waited to see whether he would go on.

"Even before we did the advice process, I would have said that was a fair call," Ben added. "Now that I listen to all this, though—" Suddenly, his shoulders sagged. "I don't think this is the first time I've hurt the company," he said. "I just think it's the first time anyone caught it."

He stared down at the stack of papers on his desk. Then he looked up at Tom. "I don't think I should be leading this facility," he said.

"Is that your decision?" Tom asked.

"Look," Ben said. "I'm a manufacturing guy. Always have been. I love it. You give me a string of machines and a sheet of specs, and I couldn't be happier. But running this facility isn't about working with machines. It's about leading people. And I've been trying to work my people like they're just another kind of machine."

"I think that's fair to say," Tom said.

"The thing is," Ben said, "you need my experience in manufacturing. But I shouldn't be leading the floor. Not just because of the agency reporting. Because of the way I've been running it up to now. So here's what I'd suggest. If you're willing to keep me, I'd like to step back. Become the machine and logistics guru, whatever name you want to put on it. And set up someone else to really lead our people. Someone who can do that better than I have."

"You have anyone in mind?" Tom asked.

"Anton did a heck of a job on the agency question," Ben said. "And you heard people talk about him. He's been thinking of ways to improve this place for years. And people like them."

"A lot of people brought up his ideas, not just their own," Tom agreed.

"Yeah," Ben said. "He's already got support, and he's not even in charge." He leaned back in his chair. "Angela made me put together a task-force for hiring. I never really let them do much but sort through resumes for me. I think we'd want to bring them in on this and get their advice before we make any final decisions. But he's who I'd tap for the job."

He met Tom's gaze. "That's if you're willing to give me another chance," he said.

"That's your call," Tom said. "It's your decision."

28.

The Final Call

The phone on Tom's desk rang. He waited through the first ring, expecting Vanessa to pick it up out in the office. By the third ring, he realized she must be gone for the day and glanced down at the caller ID. When he saw the name of the government agency that was handling their reporting error, his blood ran cold.

He reached for the phone and caught it just before it kicked to voice mail.

"Hello?" he said.

The voice on the other end was pleasant and professional: a young woman. "Hello, this is Katy Stuart," she said, and named the agency she was calling from. "I'm trying to reach Mr.—" the slight hesitation in her voice gave her away as she searched for his name. "Anderson. Tom Anderson."

"You've got him," Tom said.

"Mr. Anderson," Katy said. "We've been reviewing a case

of yours for the past few months, and I'm calling to give you our determination."

"Thank you," Tom said, trying to keep his voice neutral. He caught at a pen, to note down anything she said. "Go ahead."

"As you know," she went on, "we take any kind of reporting violation very seriously."

"I understand," Tom said. His pen twitched over the paper on his desk, but she still hadn't given him anything to go on.

"But we do understand that some mistakes are unavoidable in any process," she continued. "And we try to look with leniency on organizations that bring their mistakes to us and show willingness to rectify them."

"We have," Tom said. "We rebuilt those specs from the bottom up, and they've gone through thorough testing. And re-testing."

"I can see that from my notes," she said. "And from my conversations with Mr. Bell."

"Good," Tom said.

"Am I right that Mr. Bell works on your manufacturing floor?" Katy asked.

Tom's stomach lurched. Had the agency taken the fact that they'd allowed Anton to handle the case as a sign of disrespect? "Yes," he said, and waited for the other shoe to drop.

"He's just so well-informed on all the issues," Katy said. "It was a pleasant change."

Tom let out a silent sigh of relief.

"Usually when something goes wrong, I'm working with

executives," she went on. "Their subordinates try to prep them, but a lot of times they're coming to the party late and they never really come up to speed. There's a lot of, 'Can I call you back on that?' It bogs down the process. And then you're never sure if you can trust the answers they do bring back, since they didn't know them in the first place. But Anton was always spot on. It shortened your process by a good deal."

"That's good to hear," Tom said.

"I would have liked to give him this news first," Katy said. "But regulations specify that our determinations be delivered to the owner. You'll also receive official documents to this effect."

"All right," Tom said. He could feel his blood pressure rising.

"This is a serious violation, as I said," Katy told him. "But because you brought it to us yourself, we'll be levying a fine rather than requiring a suspension of your operations."

Tom let out a rush of breath. At least they were still in business. "Wonderful," he said.

"The fine is commensurate with an estimate of costs for clean-up based on the potential environmental impact of your violation," Katy told him. "Which we estimate at 7.8 million dollars."

Tom had dropped his hand to the page to scrawl down the number, but when he heard it, his hand froze.

"However, because you brought the issue to us before there was any environmental damage, we're suspending this fine as well. Pending no further violations during the course of the next fiscal year, it will be waived entirely."

"So," Tom said, not sure he'd heard correctly. "No fine."

"Pending no further violations during the next fiscal year," she insisted, with a government agent's precision.

"Thank you," Tom said, with feeling.

"You've got nothing to thank me for," she said. "You made the right decision, to bring this forward. If we'd discovered an error like this for ourselves, you'd be getting a very different call."

"I understand that," Tom said.

"Do you have any questions?"

Tom looked down at his notes, his mind reeling with surprise and relief. "No," he said. "Not right now."

"I have one for you, then," she said, her voice losing some of its businesslike quality as it turned curious. "I've worked on hundreds of these cases, and I've never seen another company let something like this out of the hands of the executives. Can you tell me why you did?"

The waves of stress that had hit Tom during the conversation were fading, but it took him time to collect his thoughts. A few minutes ago, he hadn't been sure himself exactly why he'd thought it was a good idea to have a member of his manufacturing team handle negotiations with a government agency that had the power to shut down his whole company.

"Well," he began. "We're a company that believes certain things about our people. We believe they're unique—not everyone should be treated exactly the same. People aren't machines. They can think and be creative and learn.

Sometimes we make mistakes, but we can be trusted to make decisions. Not just the people at the top. Everyone. No matter what their job description."

"And Anton was in manufacturing," Katy reasoned. "That's why he was so incredibly well-versed in all of the issues."

"That's right," Tom said.

"Hm," Katy said, her voice almost wistful. "I can't quite imagine that happening here. But it sounds amazing."

"Thank you," Tom said.

"Well," Katy said, snapping back into her businesslike tone. "You can look out for the official documents by mail. Anton knows how to reach me if you have any other questions. And please give my best to him. It was a pleasure to work with him. And MedTec."

Tom held the phone slightly away from his face, hardly able to believe that this was how the long-awaited conversation with the agency was going.

"Yes," Tom said. "Thank you. I will."

29.

This Place Is Special

"It's so nice to meet you," Sophia said, beaming.

Vanessa beamed back as the party swirled around them.

"I hear all of this was your idea," Sophia said, gesturing at the crowd, which included all of MedTec's people, along with their families and friends, sprawled across the sunny lawns that surrounded the MedTec building, where a tent and barbecue pit had been set up for a company picnic.

Vanessa nodded, pride gleaming in her eyes. "Tom wasn't sure about it," she said.

"I told her the bells and whistles were for companies that didn't ever let you have any fun at work," Tom admitted.

"So I told him," Vanessa said, "that we have something to celebrate here at MedTec. And it was time to celebrate it."

"And I told her it was her decision," Tom said. He smiled at the young man beside Vanessa. "And who's this?" he asked.

The boy, about fourteen or fifteen, stuck out his hand politely. "Emanuel," he said. "Nice to meet you."

"My son," Vanessa said, by way of explanation.

"Nice to meet you, too," Tom said, shaking his hand.

"I'm glad I got to see this place," Emanuel said, looking around. "My mom never liked any job before you guys came here. But now, after work, she's still smiling."

"Most days," Vanessa said, and laced her hand through her son's arm.

"I mean it," Emanuel said. "I didn't like that she used to spend so much time in places she was never happy. This place is special."

"Well, your mother's one of the reasons it's special," Tom told him.

"Yeah," Emanuel said. "But no one else ever saw that before."

As he was speaking, Anton came up beside them, hand in hand with a pretty woman in a blue dress. "Sorry to interrupt," he said.

"But his wife insisted he introduce her to the boss," the woman said, sticking out her hand. "I'm Ava," she said, when Tom took it. "So nice to meet you."

Vanessa and Emanuel headed for the beverage table.

"I've heard nothing but good things about your husband," Sophia told Ava. "He's the hero of a lot of stories Tom tells."

"Well, that's why I came over," Ava said. "I love my husband, and I always used to say, I'm lucky there are a lot of things to love about him, because try as I might, I could never get him to change. But let me tell you, now it's like living with a different man."

Anton gave her a wry smile. "Was I really that bad?"

"You weren't," Ava said. "But the job was. And it was hard to watch, for a woman who loves you." She looked back at Tom and Sophia. "He's a smart man," she said.

"He is," Tom agreed.

"Full of ideas," Ava went on. "Every night, he'd come home and tell me about them. And I'd say, 'Why don't you go in and tell your boss some of those ideas?' And he'd just say, 'No, no. They won't listen.' Until you and Jim started listening to him."

"I just wish we'd done it a lot sooner," Tom said.

"And then you had the good sense to make him the boss," Ava said. "Let him make the decisions for a change."

Anton met Tom's eyes and smiled. "Well, that's the problem," Anton said. "That's not what being the boss means around here."

"I'm afraid not," Tom said. "How is that going for you?"

Anton nodded. "Good, good," he said. "But it can be hard, sometimes. Giving everyone else on the team a chance to make the decisions."

"It sure can," Tom said.

"But still," Anton told him, "there's something I'm getting to like about it. It's like being the coach. You watch those guys on the sidelines, but they're not really on the sidelines. They're part of the game, just as much as any of the players."

"That's right," Tom said. "They are."

"You've got a lot of power when you decide who to send into the game, even if you're not the one with the ball," Anton went on. "And you know what? You watch a coach on the sidelines when one of their players makes a good play.

Sometimes I think they look even happier than the player does. That's how I feel, anyway."

"I know how you feel," Tom said.

"Well," Ava said, taking Anton's arm and glancing to the side. "It looks like we're not the only people who'd like to talk with you today."

Tom followed her gaze. Helen Harris stood a few steps away, waiting patiently. "It's so nice to meet you," Sophia told Ava as she and Anton headed toward the grill.

"Is this the receiving line?" Helen joked as she came up.

"Helen," Tom said, shaking her hand. "Thanks so much for coming. And—for everything."

Helen nodded. "I wouldn't miss it," she said. "And I actually came over to thank *you*. I know we've had our differences this year."

"But the new numbers look good, don't they?" Tom said. "You got your first dividend check?"

"I did," Helen said. "But I was always sure you and Jim would at least be able to come up with that. What I didn't expect was that you'd do it by creating a business I'm so proud to be a part of. I might not have shown it, but I always liked your ideas, even if I wasn't sure they were going to work. I've never been so glad to be wrong."

"I think we'll be throwing off some really impressive numbers when the new product comes out," Tom said.

"Yes," said Helen. "But that's not what's most impressive to me. I've never seen people this engaged or happy at a company before. Outside the executive suite, I mean. It's a good thing. And I'm glad you fought me for it."

"Well," Tom said. "Let's hope there will be less of that in the future."

Helen grinned. "Don't bet on it," she said.

As she walked away, Sophia took Tom's arm. "You know what I could really go for?" she said.

"What?" Tom asked.

"Some barbecue," she said. "Some good-old fashioned barbecue. I'm just not sure where we could get any of that around here."

"Well," Tom said, leading her over to the buffet tables, where heaps of food were piled on red and white checked cloth. "I think we might be in luck."

A few minutes later, they reached the end of the line, their plates overflowing. As Tom glanced around the tables, looking for a seat, he saw a hand waving above a familiar face.

"Jim," Sophia said at the same time.

"We've been saving these seats for you," Jim said, when they went over. Beside him, his wife, Beth, smiled. Sophia set down her plate and leaned across the table to kiss Beth on the cheek.

"Enjoying yourself?" Tom asked Jim as he sat down.

Jim nodded. "This is some delicious barbecue," he said.

"Those preliminary orders on the new product probably don't hurt your mood either," Tom joked. The figures were even better than they had hoped.

Jim smiled. "They don't hurt," he said. "But they aren't the bottom line."

"Wait," Tom said. "Let me get my phone out. I want to record you saying that."

Jim held up his hand. "All right, all right," he said. "I know sometimes it sounds like that's all I care about. And you're lucky you've got a guy like me on board."

"I'll be the first one to admit that," Tom said.

"But you've got to remember, I'm the same guy who quit our last company with you, because we both wanted something more than just a fat paycheck."

Tom could hear from the tone of Jim's voice that he'd left the jokes behind.

Jim looked around the gathered crowd. "I've never been a part of anything like this," he said. "A company where people get treated like people. Where everyone's not just the same. Where we expect people to think and learn. Where they get to make their own decisions. Not just the execs and the creative types. The guys on the line, and all the way up."

He met Tom's eyes.

"It's not just about the money for me," he said. "It never has been. I watch our bottom line because I believe in what we're creating here, and I don't want to see it end. But doing something that matters. Creating a company where people know they're part of something important. Treating them like people, not machines. Giving them a chance to contribute and learn. Seeing how they want to come in every day. Knowing that they're actually happy here—at work. That matters to me."

"That's the reason we went into business," said Tom.

"That's the bottom line," said Jim.

30.

Let Me Explain

"Welcome to MedTec," Tom said, looking out over the faces of the employees crowded into the company auditorium, where he stood on stage along with Jim, Vanessa, and Angela. "When Jim and I bought our first campus a few years ago, we had no plans to acquire another facility so soon. But you've probably heard a bit about the success of our flagship product."

A murmur of assent rippled through the room.

Tom nodded. "That's allowed us to do some things we only dreamed about doing. Including join forces with the incredible team you've already built here. And at MedTec, we've got a company culture that we think has been crucial to our success. It's called the decision-maker process."

He could see the uncertainty and skepticism in their faces. But he'd seen that before.

"It's based on a few assumptions about people," he went on. "They're different from the assumptions most companies make. A lot of companies treat their people like machines. Some companies treat their people like children."

Heads began to nod.

"At MedTec, we treat our people like people," Tom said. "We know you're unique. You're all good at different things, and you all want different things. You're creative. You can think and learn. You like a challenge. You've got something to contribute. And you're capable of making important decisions.

"Those are simple ideas," he went on. "Even common sense. But at MedTec we've found that building our business on them has changed everything about the way we do business. And now I want to hand it over to Vanessa, who's going to spend a little time unpacking what all of this means."

Vanessa smiled as he handed her the microphone.

"Okay," she said. "I know what you're thinking. Tom's obviously crazy, right?"

The room burst into laughter.

Vanessa grinned. "But that's okay," she said. "He's just the boss. Bosses are full of crazy ideas. You just keep your head down, and they'll go away. There's only one thing that stays the same at work. That's the work. And let me tell you, it is *always* the same. But that's okay. You don't come to work to be happy. That's why they call it *work*. Am I on the right track?"

The attentive faces around the room showed that she was.

Vanessa nodded and took a step closer to the edge of the stage.

"You know how I know what you're thinking right now?" she asked, looking out at the sea of faces. "Because that's what I thought, too, when I first heard these ideas. Let me explain…."

Afterword

The Decision Maker tells the story of a fictional company, but the principles were forged and tested in the real world—and not just in a small business like the one described here. Along with my partner, Roger Sant, I developed them and put them into practice at The AES Corporation, which grew to be a global power company with 27,000 people in 27 countries. I also used these principles in founding Imagine Schools, one of the largest not-for-profit networks of charter schools in the nation. The principles are simple. Some might even say common sense. But building your business on these assumptions, using these simple but powerful techniques, can transform a business—and people's lives. The next few pages (also available at *www.decisionmakerbook.com* as a slide deck to share with your colleagues) summarize the basic assumptions of a decision-maker culture, what to look for in a decision-maker, and how the advice process works.

THE
DECISI⬤N
MAKER

**Unlock the Potential of
Everyone in Your Organization,
One Decision at a Time**

DENNIS BAKKE

Hi, I'm Dennis.
I enjoy making
decisions.

Early on, I would sometimes ask others for advice, but I would make the final decision. Isn't that what leaders are supposed to do?

I soon realized that the more decisions I made, the less engaged others became, and the less ownership they had in the results. The problem was me.

The Problem I Found

Bosses are often less informed than people closer to the action.

In most organizations, bosses make all the important decisions. In fact, most people would tell you that's what leadership is. But are bosses always the best equipped to make all decisions?

The people closest to the decision know the most, and feel the most ownership.

Often, leaders aren't the closest to a situation—and they're not the people most affected by a decision. The people closest to the situation are the best informed about the personalities and factors involved. And they have the most at stake.

People are often treated like machines, not human beings.

Leaders don't often make use of the perspectives and expertise of the people who are closest to a situation. Instead, many organizations seek to control behavior through top-down leadership that enforces procedures and rules. But people aren't machines.

Result...

People don't get to make meaningful decisions at work, so they are not fully engaged.

But I believe people are capable of making decisions. My belief is grounded in the assumptions I make about people...

People Are

Unique

Creative
Thinkers

Capable of
Learning

Up for a
Challenge

Distributing the decisions more broadly and inviting more people to be part of the process will lead to more engaged people and better decisions.

It hasn't been easy to trust and empower my people to make meaningful decisions. As a boss, it's hard to let go.

And people aren't perfect.
We're all fallible — including
leaders. That's why I developed

The Decision Maker Process.

In a decision-maker organization, the leader leads by choosing a decision-maker.

The decision-maker must ask for advice.

The advice process brings multiple perspectives together to guide a successful outcome.

But the decision-maker makes the final call—and takes responsibility for it.

Choosing the Decision-Maker

The leader leads by choosing a decision-maker.

Proximity. Who's close to the issue? Are they well acquainted with the context, the day-to-day details, and the big picture?

Perspective. Proximity matters, but so does perspective. Sometimes an outside perspective can be just as valuable.

Experience. Has this person had experience making similar decisions? What were the consequences of those decisions?

Wisdom. What kinds of decisions has this person made in other areas? Were they good ones? Do you have confidence in this person?

The Advice Process

In a decision-maker culture, the decision-maker makes the final call but must ask for advice. Deciding who to get advice from can influence a successful outcome.

Get advice from people who have:

Experience. Has this person had experience with this problem? There's no teacher like experience.

Position. People in different positions see different things. The decision-maker asks a leader, a peer, someone below them in the hierarchy—and even, if circumstances warrant, experts from outside the company.

Responsibility. Decisions have consequences—and decision-makers should be held accountable for theirs. At the same time, nobody is right all the time. The most important part of any decision is that the decision-maker fully engages with the advice process, not just that he or she gets it "right."

Ownership. When people are asked for advice, they start to feel ownership. Ideally, everyone who offers advice works for the success of the project as if it were their own. The advice process isn't just about getting the right answer. It's about building a strong team and creating a process of communication that will improve all decisions in a company.

Benefits of the Advice Process

1. *Everyone becomes more engaged.*

People feel more ownership when their advice is sought.

2. *On-the-job education.*

No training can match real-time experience.

3. *Better decisions.*

When decisions involve more people who are fully engaged, an organization has a higher chance of a good outcome than it does with a conventional top-down approach.

Accountability

After the decision is made, the decision-maker follows through by communicating and measuring the results of the decision.

I've shared my story of the decision-maker process in these books...

Now, it's your turn.

Share successes and lessons

www.decisionmakerbook.com

facebook.com/decisionmakerbook

info@decisionmakerbook.com

About the author

Dennis Bakke is the co-founder of Imagine Schools. He is the author of the *New York Times* bestseller *Joy at Work: A Revolutionary Approach to Fun on the Job*. Bakke previously co-founded and served as the president and CEO of AES, a Fortune 200 global power company. He lives with his wife in Arlington, Virginia.

About the cover

A rubber-band ball bounces only when hundreds of rubber bands are stretched and bound together. Each unique rubber band is fully engaged and makes a meaningful contribution, not just the few on the top layer. The ball represents the decision-maker culture you'll discover in this book. My dream is for people at all levels of an organization to have the freedom and responsibility to make decisions that matter.

Acknowledgements

I'm forever grateful to Eileen Harvey Bakke for living each step of the journey with me at AES and Imagine Schools while attempting to make ordinary work and all of life the joy it was meant to be. In addition to being the greatest mom ever, Eileen partnered with me to create and lead Imagine Schools, a nonprofit that serves thousands of students and parents in quality public charter schools across the United States.

For editing the book, thanks to Tracy Cutchlow. For reviewing early drafts of the manuscript, thanks to Al Erisman, editor of Ethix.org, and to Bruce Baker, both of whom teach in the School of Business and Economics at Seattle Pacific University. Tim Jenkins, co-founder of Point B Management Consultants, helped make it feel more "real." Thanks for all of the advice.

For her passion to share these ideas with the world, thanks to Jenn Branstetter. Additional thanks to the Pear

Press team of Amy Hatch, Gabriel Hui-Hutter, and Danielle Zorn for introducing so many people to the decision-maker principles.

For not giving up on the radical idea that work should be fun, thanks to Mark Pearson, who published both *Joy at Work* and *The Decision Maker*.

www.decisionmakerbook.com